# GOOD STOCKS

CHEAP

Value Investing
with Confidence
for a Lifetime
of Stock Market
Outperformance

## KENNETH JEFFREY MARSHALL

McGraw Hill Education

New York   Chicago   San Francisco   Athens   London   Madrid
Mexico City   Milan   New Delhi   Singapore   Sydney   Toronto

1 2 3 4 5 6 7 8 9  LCR  22 21 20 19 18 17

ISBN      978-1-259-83607-7
MHID          1-259-83607-X

e-ISBN    978-1-259-83608-4
e-MHID        1-259-83608-8

This publication is designed to provide accurate and authoritative information in regard to the subject matter covered. It is sold with the understanding that neither the author nor the publisher is engaged in rendering legal, accounting, securities trading, or other professional services. If legal advice or other expert assistance is required, the services of a competent professional person should be sought.
— *From a Declaration of Principles Jointly Adopted by a Committee of the American Bar Association and a Committee of Publishers and Associations*

Library of Congress Cataloging-in-Publication Data

Names: Marshall, Kenneth Jeffrey.
Title: Good stocks cheap : value investing with confidence for a lifetime of stock market outperformance / Kenneth Jeffrey Marshall.
Description: 1 Edition. I New York : McGraw-Hill Education, 2017.
Identifiers: LCCN 2017002373 (print) I LCCN 2017017329 (ebook) I ISBN 9781259836084 () I ISBN 1259836088 () I ISBN 9781259836077 (hardback) I ISBN 125983607X
Subjects: LCSH: Stocks. I Value investing.
Classification: LCC HG4661 (ebook) I LCC HG4661 .M345 2017 (print) I DDC 332.63/22--dc23
LC record available at https://lccn.loc.gov/2017002373

McGraw-Hill Education books are available at special quantity discounts to use as premiums and sales promotions or for use in corporate training programs. To contact a representative, please visit the Contact Us pages us at www.mhprofessional.com.

Mississippi Mills
Public Library

To MHM.

He picked the right girl.

# CONTENTS

# PREFACE

First, my goofs. I failed to sell my Coca-Cola Company shares when they spiked past $80 in 1998. That price suggested that every man, woman, and child on earth had just pledged to drink a bathtub full of soda a week for life. And I knew that *that* hadn't happened.

Worse was Nike. I started selling it at $67 per share in 2010, concerned that its price-to-book ratio had swelled past three. But I knew that the treasured swoosh logo was carried on the company's balance sheet at precisely zero. Nike's earnings and stock price have both soared since then.

Lest my blunders be limited to consumer goods, in 2011 I passed on pipe manufacturer Mueller Industries. Its stock price had dipped following a drop in housing starts, a cyclical condition that always ends. And not only did I know that, I knew the company so well by that point that I probably could have installed one of its copper elbow fittings myself. Mueller's operating income went on to double, and its stock split.

These are some atrocities perpetrated by your author. And there were more. Sometimes I did something wrong, and other times I failed to do something right. Some were errors of commission, others errors of omission. But none of them has cost me much. They were more about upsides forgone than losses suffered.

That's a charm of value investing. It instills in one a caution that occasionally produces the unnecessary abstention, the premature sale, and the unjustified hold. But it flags disasters incomparably. For every triumph missed, a hundred disappointments are avoided. And that's a virtue of the discipline, not of the practitioner. It's available to anyone. But few ever pick up on it.

Of course, few ever pick up on just *investing*. They simply won't get it. They won't see a contribution made to a retirement account, or a deposit made at the bank, as part of a deliberate process of growing wealth. They won't view the commitment of capital today as a way to gain a larger claim on civilization's goods and services tomorrow.

Even if they buy stock in listed companies, they may not be investing. They may be merely *speculating*. I define speculating as the purchase of something now in the hope that it can be sold at a higher price later, with no consideration as to why that may be possible. Versus investing, nothing could be more different.

Of those who do understand investing, only a fraction ever get *value* investing. I define value investing as *acting on the observation of a clear difference between price and worth*.

Of the few who get value investing, only a fraction ever teach it. We could all fit in an elevator. Our lot is small because there's scant encouragement in academia to pursue the discipline.

Value investing is a subject of simplifications and approximations. It disdains the Greek letters and exactness that masquerade as a scientification of capital management. It champions the back of the envelope over the spreadsheet. It doesn't spotlight theoretical acumen, quantitative wizardry, or other hallmarks of professorial achievement. As such, it's no sure route to tenure.

So what you get in me is a subset of a subset of a subset: an investor who is a value investor who teaches value investing. Expect twists.

I am not starting a fund. I state this because a common—and valid—reason for writing is to give potential investors insight into one's thinking. My motivation comes from a different place. I have seen enough people act against their economic interests that I want a book to throw at the next flare-up. Perhaps the page will triumph where the conversation did not.

This book is about what *I* do. It's entirely my opinion, a distillation of what I see as the best practices in the discipline. It reflects my particular approach. Several parts of this approach are nonstandard. For example, I hold stocks for the long term. I don't use leverage. I don't sell stocks short. And my portfolio is concentrated, never containing more than a dozen names, and usually far fewer.

Other bona fide value investors act differently. They may churn their holdings monthly. They may borrow, short, or diversify. They would write different sorts of books.

In the end, it doesn't really matter much what my peculiarities are. Value works. Once one has committed oneself to some incarnation of a value strategy, the long-term results are likely to be good. The impact of inflections is on the margin.

Consider the way I calculate *return on capital employed*, a common metric that we'll cover. For the numerator, I use *operating income*. But many don't. They use *net income*, or *earnings before interest and taxes*. There's spirited debate on these different takes. But in context it becomes banter among the knowing. It's like beachfront homeowners comparing views. *All* the views are good.

One of the better lessons from my undergraduate economics classes was the difference between principals and agents. Principals hire agents to help them accomplish something. Agents are thought to possess special skills, connections, or other attributes that qualify them to assist.

In finance, an example of a principal/agent pairing is a high net worth individual and a registered investment advisor. Other examples are a hedge fund limited partner and a general partner, or a retail investor and a mutual fund manager.

This book is primarily for principals. It's firstly for people managing their own money. It will have little to say about how to satisfy regulators, communicate with outside investors, or other topics of interest only to agents.

Of course agents are also principals. They have their own portfolios, and often take stakes in the pools of capital that they run. In addition, the best agents run clients' money as if it were their own. So this book is useful for agents, too. But know that it is the principals that I put first.

Most readers will enjoy diving into the processes outlined in this book. But some won't. They'll find them too demanding, or tedious.

That's not a bad finding. It helps some people see that they're unlikely to stick with the value approach over the long term. That's important, because the long term is what's required to achieve real outperformance. Those turned off should instead consider low-cost index funds. These are truly useful innovations that have performed satisfactorily. They've actually beaten the returns of many otherwise high-functioning people who venture into stock picking.

Those who discover value investing tend to do so via one of two routes: trauma or exposure. Trauma, alas, is far more common. It's losing money—or not making enough—via some other strategy.

Growth, momentum, and other approaches beckon and betray. Eventually their sadism motivates investors to hunt for a better path, hopefully early enough in life to give value investing time to deliver.

The other route is exposure. It's hearing about value investing somehow, somewhere, and in such a way that it is taken seriously.

My route was the happy latter. The father of a childhood friend ran his own value stock fund. When this friend and I graduated from college in 1989, he went to work for the family firm, and I became a tiny client of its brokerage arm.

He fed me recommendations consistent with the fund's principles. I was slow to pick up on the merits of his common sense. But I've always been an empiricist. I've noticed what works, and what doesn't. I try to do the former, and to not do the latter. As the 1990s progressed, my value holdings crowded out my other, less well-considered holdings.

Then as now, theory held little interest for me except to the extent that it was practical. And toward the end of the decade, the theories behind value investing reached new heights of practicality.

The dot-com boom baffled me. At my 1999 business school reunion, previously levelheaded classmates justified that summer's high stock prices with tales of new business models and disintermediation. I was skeptical. But it was infectious. I returned to California and began working for a technology start-up.

My portfolio, however, stayed grounded. My hours may have lost their mind, but my capital kept its head. By New Year's Day my holdings were all value. I had the least fashionable brokerage account in Palo Alto.

When the bubble popped in March 2000, the merits of this discipline showed. The price of my portfolio held. The fundamentals of the companies I owned were solid. I sold nothing that year. A pandemic of euphoria had shoved me squarely into the value investing camp. There I remain.

I talk about value investing with different kinds of people. I've taught at the masters level at universities, given workshops to retail brokerage clients, and presented to alumni groups. My audiences have included a retired cardiovascular surgeon, a high school senior, a customer service representative, and a venture capital general partner. They've come from Beijing, Nairobi, Toronto, and Vaud, Switzerland. They've ranged in age from 17 to 74.

Despite this diversity, my approach is always the same. I speak plainly. I present investing as a trade, like plumbing or barbering. It's useful only if it works.

Plumbing is useful when it yields fixed sinks. Barbering is useful when it yields good haircuts. And investing is useful when it yields long-term market outperformance. Whether the investor can describe the correlation between volatility and interest rates doesn't matter any more than whether the plumber can diagram Mesopotamian irrigation, or whether the barber can draw a hair follicle. The proof is in the sink, the hair, and the return.

My plain approach carries a cost. It's that I skip some details. Experts in corporate strategy, cognitive psychology, and other disciplines that the value investing model touches on will find gaps. For example, accountants will notice that my definition of goodwill bypasses the assignment of a portion of acquisition cost to identifiable intangible assets. *Touché.*

There's a line that separates simplification from oversimplification. I've tried to draw it close to the latter without leaving the former. But the line's location varies with both the topic and the reader. On balance, I've favored clean presentations that are likely to sink in over exhaustive presentations that are likely to bore.

This book continues in the vein of my talks. To those new to finance, I hope to have written with a clarity that resonates quickly. To institutional money managers and experienced principal investors, I hope that my words lay plain a subject better known for ambiguity. Above all, I hope that this book serves as an exposure: an exposure vivid enough, reasonable enough, and engaging enough to stick. If it doesn't, there's always trauma.

# ACKNOWLEDGMENTS

If the trick to lifelong learning is to surround oneself with smarter people, I am the master. To these unwitting collaborators, I doff my cap. To wit:

At Stanford University, Hal Louchheim and Liz Frith for seeing potential in my vision of an all-comers value investing course, and to the band of San Francisco Bay Area believers that proved them right; and to Teresa Kpachavi and Matt Hein for moving the course online so ably that it's now attracted students from all but one continent;

At the Stockholm School of Economics, professors Karl-Olof Hammarkvist, Magnus Dahlquist, and Bo Becker for a *varmt välkomnande*;

Joy Tutela at the David Black Agency;

Donya Dickerson and Knox Huston at McGraw-Hill;

Friends who heaped expertise and enthusiasm my way, including Upal Basu, Larry Gorman, Allison Joyce, Mary Komatsu, Yun Hao Lo, Hari Ramachandra, Patti Rice, Benjamin Schmid, Jay Siva, Tom Svedenstrand, Mikael Tarnawski-Berlin, Janardhanan Vembunarayanan, and Pierre Wong;

The magnificent Mitchells—brothers Andy and Bill—both writers and value investors like me, but far more personable;

And dear mother and father, entrepreneurs' entrepreneurs, for—among much else—teaching me to think like an owner and to write like I mean it.

As with any work such as this, full responsibility for errors must be borne by the author. May their insignificance be matched only by their innocence.

# INTRODUCTION

This book puts forth a model. It's a model used to vet stock investment ideas from a value investing perspective. Which is useful, because that's the perspective that delivers the highest returns over time.

The model does three things. First, it makes it *likely* that one will make investments that, over a lifetime, produce *above-market* rates of return. Second, the model makes it *unlikely* that one will make investments that deliver *below-market* rates of return. So far, so good.

Unfortunately, the model also introduces the possibility that one will *not* make investments that *would have* delivered above-market rates of return. It will sometimes urge one to say *no* when one could have said *yes*. It delivers particularly weird verdicts on financial institutions and utilities, sorts of businesses that it's bad at assessing. But as will be made clear, one happily accepts these pitfalls in exchange for the first two benefits.

The model begins with three steps. Each step is a question that we ask of the proposed investment. First, do I understand it? Second, is it good? And third, is it inexpensive?

The three steps are sequential. They're to be answered in order. And each must be answered with a yes in order to move on to the next. If an investment isn't understood, there's no point in seeing if it's good. If it's not good, there's no point in seeing if it's inexpensive. The moment one gets a no, one can reject the idea. So the model sets a high standard for one's investments. They must be understandable, good, *and* inexpensive.

There's much more to the model. We'll develop it naturally over the coming chapters. Any motivated person is capable of mastering all of it regardless of education, profession, or experience.

The model pulls from three disparate disciplines: finance, strategy, and psychology. The first discipline, finance, reveals which companies have been operationally successful and are underpriced. It's accounting, plus some calculations based on that accounting. It's a quantitative activity that happily requires nothing more complicated than simple math.

The second discipline, strategy, shows which companies with successful *pasts* promise to have successful *futures*. It's qualitative. It involves thinking about what sets a company apart from its peers, and picturing it years onward.

The third, psychology, is about the restraint necessary to reject the misjudgments that naturally arise from one's inborn biases. Humans think funny. It's not that we're silly or wrong. It's just that we're *people*. To be mindful of the bad calls we're likely to make is to maximize the chance that we'll catch them before they hurt us.

In short, our approach is interdisciplinary. It's interdisciplinary not because we need to show the world how Renaissance we are. It's interdisciplinary because *it has to be*. Someone good at crunching numbers but ignorant of cognitive biases has a limitation. A good corporate strategist who can't read a financial statement stands no chance. And a psychologist who can't recognize strategic advantage won't beat the market.

This is why successful value investors routinely call on all three of these disciplines. But this is easy to miss. Many investing books focus on financial analysis. Some add competitive strategy. But psychology tends to be a stand-alone topic. I think that this is because professional value investors—particularly those who write books—are already so practiced at self-discipline that they don't see psychology as a discrete subject worthy of attention. I do.

This book cites specific corporations to provide examples. They're reliable as of this writing. But businesses change. Scandals emerge. Strategies shift. Companies cited for one characteristic in these pages may come to be known for an altogether different one in the future. Some changes will be spectacular and some will be shameful, but all are unforeseen by your author. Readers are therefore advised to make sure that this is the most recent edition of this book. That should lessen the chance that what was timely in the year of writing seems odd in the year of reading.

# PART I

# FOUNDATIONS

## CHAPTER 1

# The Quiet Outperformer

Value investing is an investment *strategy*. It's a *way* that wealth is deployed in pursuit of a return.

Value investing outperforms other strategies over time. Studies show this. Not some of the studies. *All* of the studies.

Wading through these studies takes some time and requires the unsocial bent that makes swimming in academese fun. But a good roundup can be found in a paper called *What Has Worked in Investing*, published by the New York investment firm Tweedy, Browne.[1] It's dated and stiff, but ever wonderful:

http://www.goodstockscheap.com/1.1.htm

A regular reader of business news can be excused for underestimating value investing's efficacy. After all, other approaches   growth, emerging markets, high frequency trading—appear in the headlines more often. So if value investing works so well, why don't we hear more about it?

There are two reasons. First, the strategy is underrepresented in new offerings. Professionals just don't launch value funds much. That means less media coverage. The strategies we hear the most about are the ones that want to be noticed. They're the ones that may have performed best last quarter, or that play on some current theme in geopolitics or technology. They're the approaches around which investment managers find it easiest to raise money, the ones on which new funds are based. They're *loud*. They naturally force their way to cable news shows, blogs, and newspapers.

By contrast, value investing is downright *demure*. It's not clamoring for the public's cash. Some of its practitioners stop accepting new clients. Others go as far as to close their funds, return outsized gains to investors, retire from outside money management, and recede from view. They're actively *not* raising capital.

It's understandable why ambitious money managers are unmotivated to choose value as their strategy. For one, the value approach can take some time to play out. A share bought for less than it's worth should rise in price, but the timetable by which it will rise is unknowable. Stated differently, value investors know *what's* going to happen, but they don't know *when*. As such, value managers rarely get instant gratification. Patience is required. This can turn off young guns.

Another reason managers don't start value funds is because of compensation norms in the investment industry. Value funds are often simple. They're frequently long-only equity funds, just buying stocks with their own money. They typically pay managers 1 percent of assets under management per year.

But complicated funds often pay more. A typical long/short equity fund—that is, a fund that both buys stocks and bets that other stocks will go down—pays managers 2 percent of assets under management per year, plus 20 percent of any gain above some hurdle. Those are bigger numbers. They look bright and shiny to those hustling out of business school.

The odd thing is that on average and over time, the simple funds perform better than the complicated funds. That is, managers that *succeed* doing something *plain* are paid less than those that *fail* at doing something *fancy*. To fully grasp just how bizarre this is, consider an analogy.

In gymnastics, extra points are awarded for difficulty. Competitors can incorporate challenging elements into their routines with confidence, knowing that they'll be subsidized for their trickier skills. This has real utility. For example, a gymnast can earn extra points for executing an Arabian double front, a sort of half twist with two somersaults. It's hard, but it's beautiful. Spectators benefit, treated as they are to the sight of an ambitious tumbling pass. And the sport of gymnastics benefits, as its artistic and athletic boundaries widen.

The investment management industry also awards extra points for difficulty. Professionals are compensated more for trying something harder. But on balance they fail. And much pain comes from this. Sustained underperformance costs clients money. Managers' Arabian double fronts result in face-plants, not sometimes, but *usually*.

Consider a different comparison. Imagine two airlines offering to fly you from San Francisco to San Diego. Airline A offers to fly you normally. Airline B offers to fly you backward and upside down, and to charge you more for the privilege. Absurd, right?

And yet that's *exactly* the investment management industry setup. The wackiest pilots are paid premiums for their daring.

Now on some level, flying backward and upside down has a nice ring to it. It sounds exciting. And if the goal is to *get excited*, airline B has its appeal. But that isn't the goal. The goal is to *get to San Diego*.

What happens in investment management is that people forget that the goal is to get to San Diego, and get consumed instead with the prospect of flying backward and upside down. Folks forget that the point is to generate long-term excess returns, and come to think that it's to gain exposure to certain industries, strategies, or markets. They're misled into redefining the objective.

Another reason we don't hear more about value investing is that it's a quiet activity by nature. Buying shares on the open market and holding them for years is simply not an attention-getting activity.

By contrast, consider venture capital. When a venture capital fund invests in a startup, the event is often trumpeted. Take Airbnb's $100 million fund-raising during the fourth quarter of 2015. It was splashed across the pages of the *Wall Street Journal*,[2] *Fortune*,[3] and the *Financial Times*.[4] But value investing firm Gardner Russo & Gardner's investment in beer company Anheuser-Busch InBev during the same period went largely unreported, despite the fact that it was twice as large.[5]

This epitomizes a perverse truth. There's an inverse relationship between *performance* and *visibility*. The approaches poised to disappoint get attention, while value investing outshines unseen.

## Summary

1. Value investing performs better over time than other strategies.
2. Value investing's efficacy is underreported, and will remain so.

## CHAPTER 2

# Why Stocks?

Most value investors focus on *stocks*. Stocks are also called *shares* or *equity*.

Most value investors favor *public* company stocks specifically. These shares trade on exchanges. They're *listed*.

Listed stocks constitute an *asset class*. They're a group of securities whose prices tend to move together in response to events.

There are plenty of asset classes besides listed stocks. Bonds, for example. Bonds are debt. While stocks are business ownership interests, bonds are IOUs. Bonds can be issued by countries, cities, and corporations of all sizes.

There are other asset classes as well: currencies, like the euro and the Australian dollar; commodities like corn and silver; and stocks in privately held companies, like start-ups. So why do value investors prefer listed stocks?

Because listed stocks return better than anything else over time. We choose public equities to tilt probability in our favor.

How well do listed stocks do? Quite well. The S&P 500 Index reflects the return from investing in the public equities of large American companies. Since I was born in 1967, it has returned an average of just over 10 percent per year including dividends. That's a lot. It turned $10,000 on my day of birth into over $1,000,000 at the end of 2015.

It's easy to see why listed stocks outperform bonds. Bonds represent a promise to repay some fixed amount plus interest. The money that can come out of a bond investment is thereby limited. It's limited to the principal, or the amount originally loaned, plus interest.

Sometimes a bond's interest rate is locked. Other times it varies, set at some spread over a fluctuating benchmark. If the benchmark rises, bond interest payments can rise. But they don't soar just because an issuer thrives. No company decides to pay its bondholders a bonus. And the loaned amount—the principal—doesn't go up at all. That's why there's a ceiling on how much bonds can return. It's why bonds are called a *fixed income* security.

Stocks have no ceiling. Businesses don't have a set limit on how well they can do. They can earn customers' trust, introduce new products, enter new markets, source better, and increase earnings for decades. There's no guarantee that they will, but they *can*. That's why stocks perform better over time. They're nothing less than claims on ever-growing earnings. They offer *ceiling-free upside*.

Like bonds, currencies also have limited potential as an investment. This is for two reasons. First is inflation. Inflation erodes the purchasing power of cash over time.

Consider the Balboa Bar, an ice cream treat from my Southern California boyhood. It's a rectangular block of vanilla ice cream on a stick, dunked in a pot of molten chocolate, and then smeared in topping. Connoisseurs choose crushed peanuts on one side and chocolate sprinkles on the other.

My family moved to Southern California in 1979. That summer, this masterpiece cost $1.25. Thirty-seven years later in 2016, I bought one for $3.75. That comes out to an annual average price increase just above 3 percent. In other words, the money required to buy one Balboa Bar in 1979 bought only a third of one in 2016. Time had made the dollar worth less.

Even if I had deposited my 1979 $1.25 in an interest-bearing savings account, the 2016 balance would have bought less than one Balboa Bar. Why?

Taxes. Earned interest is taxable income. If I paid an average of 50 percent of my income in taxes every year—which summing California and federal rates is roughly right—I would have had to have earned twice the rate of inflation just to stay even. But my bank's average interest rate was much less than that.

This was not some quirk of my bank. It offered typical savings account rates. And United States inflation between 1979 and 2016 averaged around 3 percent per year,[1] just like the Balboa Bar. It's representative.

The second reason currencies offer modest returns is the nature of the foreign exchange market. It's big. It's the largest financial market in the world by volume, involving millions of participants. Mispricings disappear in a flash. Opportunities to profitably trade one currency for another are therefore scarce.

Commodities also fall short as a long-term investment. Over decades, the prices of crops and metals do nothing more than track inflation. And when one takes into account carrying costs—the fees involved in moving and warehousing copper, for example—returns can actually lag inflation.

Unlisted stocks—ownership interests in privately held companies—also perform modestly on average. This may be hard to believe. Stories about stockholders in start-ups getting rich abound. For example, early investors in WhatsApp earned an average annual return of approximately 600 percent when Facebook acquired it in 2014.[2]

But for every WhatsApp, there are a hundred Firepads. You haven't heard of Firepad? That's the technology start-up that I went to work for after my 1999 business school reunion. Despite the best efforts of my colleagues there—many of whom went on to deserved success elsewhere—Firepad never soared.

The history of unlisted stock performance suffers from *selection bias*. The successes are trumpeted, but the far more numerous failures are muted. There's no central authority through which losses must be disclosed, so silence is easy to maintain. This applies to private company holdings in all forms including angel investing, venture capital, and private equity. The few home runs set high expectations, and the many strikeouts disappear.

This bias creeps into official statistics. In early 2015, the National Venture Capital Association said that "venture capital outperformed the DJIA, NASDAQ Composite, and S&P 500 during the 10-, 15-, and 20-year horizons."[3]

This claim was based on the U.S. Venture Capital Index® published by Cambridge Associates. Cambridge is a respected outfit. But it says that it gets its data from "the fund managers themselves. Unlike other data providers, Cambridge Associates does not use

Freedom of Information Act (FOIA) requests, regulatory filings, manager surveys, or press 'scrapings' to obtain information."[4]

Self-reporting of this sort can yield shinier numbers than does compulsory disclosure. Imagine if selection bias applied to our perception of public company stock performance. It could be as if the S&P 500 were composed entirely of a rotating cast of the index's five best performing stocks each year.

In 2014, the S&P 500 returned 11 percent.[5] But if we simply throw out the 495 laggards, it was 101 percent.

To be sure, there will be years when other asset classes outperform listed stocks. Gold did in 2010.[6] In other years the best-returning holding may be the Indian rupee, Brazilian government bonds, or stock in a private company. And there's always the outlying practitioner that seems able to crank out exceptional performance from some peripheral asset class consistently. But on average and over time, it's exchange-traded shares that do best for most people.

While asset classes other than listed equities can disappoint *investors*, they can delight *managers*. Heads of bond, currency, commodity, private equity, and venture capital funds can get rich. Stories circulate about their successes. But such tales aren't born of the performance of the asset class. They're born of generous compensation arrangements and ballooning fund sizes, not of high returns enjoyed by outside investors. They're about agents, not principals. They shouldn't color one's frame of reference.

Asset classes other than listed equities are not without social utility. Municipal bonds finance the construction of needed urban infrastructure. Venture capital backs the development of medical breakthroughs. Crop futures control price uncertainty for farmers. But they're securities from which it's harder to squeeze outsized returns.

Value investors tend to look at listed stocks differently. We don't think of them as electronic symbols that pop up or down in price over the next week, day, or hour. We think of them as *stakes in businesses*. This perspective makes investing a deliberate, considered activity. It's about *buying businesses*.

To drive this home, we often adopt the perspective that we're buying *entire* businesses. Our approach is therefore the same whether we're buying 100 shares of a company or 100 percent of a company. To analyze an investment, we start by analyzing a *business*.

This approach is called *fundamental analysis*. It's looking at a company's financial statements, strategic positioning, and other firm-specific factors. It has little use for stock price charts or macroeconomics.

Our primary data source in fundamental analysis is annual reports. These are the magazine-like documents that listed companies send to shareholders every year. They can be downloaded for free from company websites. But they're often over 100 pages long, festooned as they are with infographics, logos, and executive photographs. How can we navigate them efficiently?

A good rule of thumb is *the prettier the page, the less useful it is*. Zoom right past the bar charts, CEO letters, and world maps. The meat of an annual report often begins with the consolidated financial statements.

The prominence of pages allocated to a subject in an annual report is unrelated to the importance of that subject. It reflects only the prominence of pages allocated to that subject. *We* decide what matters.

Consider General Motors Company. Its 2014 annual report is 135 pages long. It starts with a dozen pages of pictures and stories about a Chevrolet-owning equestrian in Colorado, a repositioning of the Cadillac brand, and donations of soccer balls to kids in conflict zones.[7] Is this information paramount to the value investor? No. Is it pointless? Also no. But it doesn't merit the attention that its premium placement suggests.

American companies file a delightfully stripped-down version of their annual report called a 10-K. It's a black-and-white affair, mercifully devoid of product shots and pie charts. Non-U.S. companies that have stock trading on American exchanges file a similar report called a 20-F.

Forms 10-K and 20-F are also downloadable from company websites, or from the website of the Securities and Exchange Commission at www.sec.gov. Some American companies even do us the service of baking their 10-Ks right into their annual report.

There's no shortage of online data services that offer the same information that 10-Ks, 20-Fs, and annual reports do, and often in more digestible formats. Why would we then want to read things the old-fashioned way?

For two reasons. First, annual reports are—on the margin—more reliable. Online data services are publishers. They're shielded. In the United States, they're protected by the First Amendment to the Constitution. In Canada, they're protected by the Canadian Charter of Rights and Freedoms; in Germany by the Basic Law; and in many other countries by similar freedom of expression safeguards. If an online data service makes a mistake, it may lose some subscribers.

By contrast, corporations are required to file annual reports that are accurate under penalty of law. If they willfully publish a falsehood, an executive could *go to jail*. Who's likely to take a sharper pencil to their calculations, the publisher or the CFO?

Second, online data services summarize narrative portions of annual reports. This requires them to interpret. And this can lead to distortions, however unintended. The value investor prefers to get as close to the root source as possible. We want to hear it from the horse's mouth. *We'll* do the interpreting.

Quarterly reports are also useful, but less so than annual reports. This is because quarterlies are not written with the same level of scrutiny. It's not that they're sloppy. It's just that they're not *audited*. They haven't been picked through by an outside public accountancy to confirm the integrity of their figures. Audits aren't perfect, but they do provide an additional layer of assurance.

Another reason that quarterlies are less useful is that the fourth quarter of a fiscal year can serve to mop up estimates from the prior three quarters. Numbers presented for a 3-month period are therefore not as solid as numbers prepared for a 12-month period.

But quarterlies do have their place. As will be shown later, they're best used as a source for numbers that need to be timely more than they need to be audited.

In the United States, quarterly reports are available in a straightforward form called a 10-Q. Like 10-Ks, 10-Qs can be downloaded for free.

An additional document of great use with an American company is the *proxy statement*. It's available for free download from a company's website shortly before its annual shareholders meeting. It contains information on executive compensation, fees paid to the members of the board of directors, and potential conflicts of interest.

Ideally this data would be included in annual reports. In many other countries, it is.

Another data source is investor relations departments. These teams answer questions from actual and potential shareholders. They're best approached by e-mail, with clear questions that have factual answers. Smaller companies have their CFOs perform this function, or farm it out to specialized investor relations firms.

I have found investor relations people to range from helpful to unresponsive. The best ones are businesslike. They answer quickly and thoroughly. Lesser ones do less. But an imperfect reply is useful information by itself. *How* investor relations answers questions *is part of the answer.*

It may seem unusual that value investors' most reliable sources of information are costless. But they are. This clashes with images of the serious equity trader surrounded by computer monitors fed by real-time data services. But as with so much in value investing, free and simple emerges as better than pricey and complicated.

## Summary

1. Value investors focus on listed stocks because they return best over time.
2. Stocks are business ownership interests.
3. Intelligent stock investing begins with fundamental analysis.
4. The most reliable, free data source for fundamental analysis is annual reports.

## CHAPTER 3

# Price and Value Are Different

Aqua Sphere is a brand of Italian swim goggles. Compared to classic swim goggles, they look funny. Instead of the common double-cup design, they have a single broad frame that embraces the face with a flanged silicone skirt. They look like a pair of ski goggles flattened.

To the swimmer, this design has advantages. The force exerted by the straps is comfortably distributed over a wider area of the face. The soft grab of the skirt minimizes leakage. The flatness reduces drag. And if the swimmer in the next lane errantly bats the frame, a cup doesn't flip over to drive a convex solid into the eyeball.

For these reasons, many swimmers prefer Aqua Spheres to classic swim goggles. They're superior.

I bought my pair of Aqua Spheres for $23 at Sports Basement, a discount sporting goods store in San Francisco. But 10 blocks away at a triathlon boutique, the same model costs $30. Of course, both work the same. Same comfort, same watertightness, same stream-lined shape. Perhaps obviously, price has no effect on quality.

Now imagine a situation where this highly functional product starts to rise in price. Suddenly, no Aqua Sphere goggle is available anywhere in California for less than $35.

Swimmers start to rationalize this. *Because they're made in Genoa. Because Olympians use them.* Rumor takes hold. *Because they're going to stop making them.* Aqua Sphere develops a rarified, elite reputation.

Bloggers pick up on this sentiment. They seize on previously over-looked virtues. *They're tested in the Mediterranean. Royals love them.* Fitness product reviewers uncover links between the single-frame construction and sexual magnetism. *Supermodels have a different pair for each swimsuit.* Demand soars. Unemployment in Genoa disappears.

Now imagine the opposite. Instead of rising in price, Aqua Spheres *plunge* in price. First, the triathlon boutique matches Sports Basement at $23. Then the boutique stops carrying them entirely, closing out its remaining inventory at $19. Aqua Sphere goggles start showing up in drugstore bargain bins with red $9.99 price tags slapped on the mirrored plastic lenses.

The chatter among swimmers changes. *They're not classic. They look weird.* The Salvation Army notes a curious spike in Italian swim goggle donations. Suddenly, no one wants to be caught dead in those *things.*

Silly? Well, to the extent that sports products follow fashion trends, the scenario is conceivable. Demand for particular models of swimsuits, for example, certainly ebbs and flows with changing tastes.

But performance swim goggles may be more of a technical product. They're judged on their merits. Aqua Spheres have an objective set of characteristics that most competent swimmers appreciate. They're more comfortable. They leak less. They're streamlined. For these straightforward reasons, they're exceptional.

What about companies? Are they subject to fashion trends, or are they judged on their merits? Surely they too have characteristics that speak to their value. And yet sentiment often swings because of stock price movements.

Some companies are superior. They have outstanding operating results, solid strategic positionings, and a shareholder-friendly orientation. Often these companies are priced fairly. But sometimes, their price soars. Others times, it plunges. But their value isn't impacted by price swings any more than Aqua Spheres get leakier when they go on sale.

This notion is central to our discipline. Value investing has at its core the fundamental belief that price and value are *different.* Price is what something can be purchased or sold for at a given point in time. Price fluctuates.

Value, by contrast, is what something is *worth.* It fluctuates *less.*

To the value investor, price says *nothing* about value. Only *fundamental analysis* speaks to value. With swim goggles, fundamental analysis is testing comfort, watertightness, and drag. With companies, it's testing historic operating performance, strategic positioning, and shareholder-friendliness. Price doesn't register. It affects *when* to buy, but not *what* to buy.

It's easy to miss this distinction. In popular media, price is regularly mistaken for value. For example, Apple's stock price hit a new high in late 2014. London's *Telegraph* newspaper shouted, "Apple is now worth more than $700bn," calling it, "the most valuable company in the world."[1]

Was Apple really *worth* $700 billion? Or was that merely Apple's *price*? It was the latter. It *may* also have been the former, but it was *certainly* the latter.

The value investor's decoupling of price and value runs counter to a principle from economics called the *efficient market hypothesis*. It holds that the price of something *is* its worth. The efficient market hypothesis is premised on *rationality*. That's the idea that people weigh costs and benefits before acting in a market that, as a consequence, generates accurate prices.

Value investors concede that over time, the average price of a stock mirrors its average worth. But at a single *point* in time, it may not. And those single points are enough to shatter the efficient market hypothesis. The moments when price is far away from value are when the value investor acts.

Most people think that a high and rising stock price evidences a high-value company, and that a low and falling stock price evidences a low-value company. They take price as an *indicator* of quality.

Value investors don't suffer from this delusion. We use fundamental analysis to arrive at some notion of *intrinsic value*. Intrinsic value is our measure of a company's worth.

Determining intrinsic value is an objective process. But it requires some judgments. I find many of these judgments difficult to make. For example, there's a number we'll cover called *excess cash*. It's cash that a company *has* but doesn't *need*.

Some value investors assume that *all* cash is excess. The thinking goes that if the cash were needed, it wouldn't be cash anymore. It would have been used to *buy something*.

Others think the opposite. They assume that *all* of the cash is required absent evidence to the contrary. They believe that a cash hoard benefits a company by, at a minimum, scaring off potential competitors.

I often can't tell. So I sometimes calculate two sets of numbers. One assumes that all of the cash is excess, and one assumes that *none* of the cash is excess. I wind up with two intrinsic values that bookend a *range*.

Working with ranges turns out to be sufficient. If a good company is priced well *below* the *lower* end of my range, it's inexpensive. I buy it. If it's priced wildly *above* the *upper* end of my range, it's expensive. I may sell it. My inability to pin down an exact intrinsic value doesn't emerge as a limitation. It might in a PhD dissertation, but it doesn't if I'm just trying to figure out whether to buy or sell stock.

A price is not inexpensive just because it dropped. If the price of a stock is 50 percent below its high for the year, that's evidence that the price of the stock is 50 percent below its high for the year. It says nothing else. Similarly, a price is not high just because it soared. An extreme price movement may awaken us to an opportunity to analyze a company, but other than that, it's uninformative.

Note how *different* the value investing view on price is. It's an *offer*. We can take it. Or we can not take it. It doesn't *teach* us anything. If it's outside our range of intrinsic value, we don't suddenly question our analysis. We pause, gather ourselves, and see if there's something smart to do.

## Summary

1. Some companies are superior.
2. Superior companies are worth buying at some price, but not at any price.
3. Price and value are commonly conflated.
4. Investors who distinguish between price and value enjoy a rare advantage.

## CHAPTER 4

# Measuring Performance

Correctly measuring one's own investment returns may seem to be an insultingly basic topic to address. It's so *rote*. Professional fund managers in particular may be quite comfortable with their tried-and-true methods, thank you very much. But practices turn out to be so disparate, and the chance of self-deception so high, that it's worth reviewing.

Calculating one's historic performance correctly is useful. It provides a baseline, as well as a template for tracking future returns. Plus it reveals whether or not there's any room for improvement.

The calculation should be honest. It should be harsh in the way that a scale is harsh with a dieter. Brokerage statements are confusing, peppered with the obscurities for which financial institutions are famous. But they do contain the data needed to make one's own calculations.

I measure my own performance in three steps. First, I measure my percentage return for each individual year. Second, I calculate my yearly average rate. Third, I compare that average to a standard.

First, I calculate each year's return. For each year I want to know how much I *made* relative to how much I *managed*. How much I made is the *numerator*, the top part of a fraction. How much I managed is the *denominator*, the bottom. Both are expressed in currency. When I divide the numerator by the denominator, I get a percentage that equals my return for that year.

The numerator is the sum of four parts: capital appreciation, realized gains, dividends, and interest.

First is *capital appreciation*. It's how much a stockholding went up—or down—in market price. I calculate it for each individual stockholding that, at the *end* of the year, I still owned.

If I carried the stockholding *into* the *beginning* of the year, I subtract the year's beginning price from the year's closing price. I do this for the entire holding, to capture the number of shares that I owned. If I owned 1,000 shares of a company that began the year priced at $100 per share and ended the year priced at $120 per share, I would subtract $100,000 from $120,000.

The year's beginning price—$100 in the example above—comes from the *prior* year's brokerage statement. It's the prior year's closing price. Using it is better than looking up the price of a stock on the first day of the year, because that could be the closing price *after* the year's first day of trading. I want the price *before* trading starts for the year.

If I bought the stockholding *during* the year, I subtract the total purchase price—including commission—from the year's closing price.

The second part of the numerator is *realized gains*. It's like capital appreciation, but for stockholdings that I *sold* during the year. If I carried the stockholding into the beginning of the year, I subtract the year's beginning price from the selling price net of commission. If I bought the holding during the year, I subtract the purchase price including commission from the selling price net of commission.

The third part of the numerator is total dividends received during the year. That's easy, since it's printed right on the brokerage statement.

Some governments withhold portions of dividends paid as taxes. For example, France withholds 30 percent.[1] If one share of a French company pays a dividend of 10, but 3 is withheld and there's no easy way to reclaim it (there isn't), then the right dividend to count is 7. The 10 is fiction.

Nothing against France. Other countries also make reclaiming withholdings a chore. To be sure, there is a prescribed way to do it. It starts with filling out forms 5000 and 5001 from France's *Ministère du Budget des Comptes publics de la Fonction Publique*. But the process is neither certain nor fast.

The fourth part of the numerator is interest. There are two sorts. One is interest earned on cash that was eventually used to buy stock during the year. Next is interest earned on cash *received* from stock *sold* during the year.

As I write, interest earned on cash in American brokerage accounts is near zero. It's not worth counting. But in a higher rate environment—like back when Balboa Bars cost $1.25 in 1979—it's *very* worth counting. Such times could return. Good formulas are built to accommodate such eventualities.

The total numerator is capital appreciation, plus realized gains, plus dividends, plus interest.

This way of calculating the numerator is better than simply subtracting the January 1 market price of a portfolio from the December 31 market price of a portfolio. It's better because some money may have been withdrawn during the year. An individual investor may have withdrawn cash to buy a house. An institutional money manager may have used cash to pay redemptions. It would be silly to count such withdrawals as reducing returns. By the same token, it would be silly to see *deposits* as *increasing* returns. Our method avoids both problems.

The denominator is how much money was managed during the year. Formally, that's called *assets under management*. It's the financial base that yields the capital appreciation, the realized gains, the dividends, and the interest.

Picture an orchard of fruit trees. The harvest is the numerator. The acreage is the denominator.

The denominator is the sum of two parts. First is any stockholdings carried into the year, at the beginning of the year's price. Second is any cash used to purchase stocks during the year.

Dividing the numerator by the denominator gives the return for the year. Specifically, it gives the *total return* (Figure 4.1). *Total* indicates that dividends are included in the numerator.

A total return figure is useful if it's calculated with integrity. There are two ways to ensure that it is. First, include everything. An investor with multiple brokerage accounts should lump them all together, even the ones that did poorly.

Second, pick the actual investing start date. One shouldn't cherry-pick the day that happens to coincide with when a portfolio started taking off in price.

```
      Capital appreciation
  +   Realized gains
  +   Dividends
  +   Interest
  _____    = Total return

  Assets under management
```

**FIGURE 4-1:  Calculation of total return**

My second step in measuring performance is calculating my yearly average rate. The average is more important than the return from any single year because what counts is *long-term* performance. It counts because hopefully one will live for a period of time that bears more resemblance to the long term than to a single year.

Three years of total returns is the minimum for making an average calculation meaningful.

My last three drives from Palo Alto to Mountain View took 12, 11, and 22 minutes respectively. So my average was 15 minutes. That's the kind of average encountered in daily life. It's called the *arithmetic mean*. It's the sum of all data points divided by the number of data points.

But arithmetic mean isn't what we use with returns, because it fails to capture the *compounding effect of growth*. What we want instead is called the *geometric mean*. It's also referred to as the *compound annual growth rate*, or *CAGR*.

The geometric mean is the rate that, if applied identically every year, would achieve *smoothly* what was actually achieved *bumpily*.

Spreadsheets provide built-in functions for calculating the geometric mean. In Microsoft Excel, Google Sheets, and Apache OpenOffice, the function is called GEOMEAN.

Pretend that my driving times were actually my returns from three consecutive years. That is, assume that I had total returns of 12 percent one year, 11 percent the next, and 22 percent the next. GEOMEAN tells me that my average was 14 percent:

http://www.goodstockscheap.com/4.1.xlsx

Some spreadsheet geometric mean functions can't handle negative numbers. They may not work if the data includes a year with, for example, a negative 10 percent return.

Working around this problem is easy. Simply add 100 percent to each year's return. The negative 10 percent year would then become 90 percent. Then use the geometric mean function. Subtract 100 percent from the result. That's the yearly average rate.

My third step in measuring performance is comparing my average to a standard. There are two kinds of standards: *relative* and *absolute*.

The relative standard is an index, like the S&P 500 Total Return. This index returned 2.1 percent in 2011, 16.0 percent in 2012, and 32.4 percent in 2013. The geometric mean of these three figures is 10.3 percent, as GEOMEAN makes clear. So for this three-year period, 10.3 percent is the *benchmark*.

If one's yearly average return over this same three year period was 5 percent, one lagged this benchmark. Specifically, one lagged it by 530 *basis points*. If it was 14 percent, one beat it by 370 basis points.

Why don't we just say 3.7 percent? To avoid a misunderstanding. That could be read to mean 10.3 percent plus the quantity 10.3 percent *times* 3.7 percent. That would equal 10.3 percent plus 0.4 percent, which is 10.7 percent. But we don't want to *take* 3.7 percent *of* 10.3 percent. We want to *add* 3.7 percent *to* 10.3 percent. That's 14 percent. Saying *basis points* makes this clear.

The other standard is absolute. It's a fixed percentage, like 10 percent. The absolute standard ignores what indices did.

Proponents of the absolute approach note that only positive returns have utility. After all, minuses can't be spent. A 6 percent loss isn't useful, the thinking goes, just because the index lost 8 percent.

Advocates of the relative approach counter that the market provides a tailwind that naturally causes positive returns. Failing to recognize this, the thinking goes, is to ignore a general upward trend in stock prices. A 22 percent total return may sound impressive, but less so if the index returned 21 percent.

Stated differently, covering 100 meters in an airport in 10 seconds sounds like an Olympic sprint qualifying time, provided that the moving sidewalk is ignored.

Much debate on the relative approach centers on the selection of the benchmark. It's one thing to pick a broad market index like the

S&P 500 or the Dow Jones Industrial Average. They're designed to reflect the general economy. But it's quite another to compare returns to a tailored index that seems designed to do something else.

The Harlem Globetrotters is an American exhibition basketball team famous for their trick shots and funny passes. They're about entertainment, not competition. To showcase their stunts, they travel with an opposing team called the Washington Generals.

The Washington Generals play uninspired basketball. They're bad, on purpose. Their goal is to *lose*.

Some benchmarks seem like the Washington Generals of investing. They're designed to be beaten. Stated differently, there are *so many* specialized indices to choose from that one is certain to beat *one* of them. One benchmark provider offers over 180,000 global equity indexes.[2]

But finding a Washington Generals is not the value investor's goal. If one chooses to benchmark, one should pick a standard index. Do so once, and stick with it. Don't switch.

I prefer the relative approach. I benchmark my own performance against the S&P 500 Total Return. This index includes dividends, as it should, since my own return includes dividends. My opinion is that a skilled value investor can, over time, beat this benchmark by an average of around 500 basis points per year.

Of course, my preference isn't that meaningful. The longer the time period, the less it matters whether one uses the relative or absolute approach. This is because with each additional year, the average return of a broad market index comes closer to the sort of fixed percentage that an absolutist would pick as a standard. So it doesn't much matter.

What does matter is long-term results. Returns for an individual year mean little. And returns for shorter periods mean even less. It's pointless to measure performance over quarters or months. Such periods capture wild price moves that reflect others' elation and panic, not one's own ability. Tracking them can even be counterproductive by giving rise to short-term targets pursued to the detriment of long-term returns.

Earlier I noted how some governments withhold dividend taxes, and that absent bureaucracy navigation talent, only dividends *net* of such withholdings belong in a numerator. Besides that, the returns we've discussed are *pretax*. This is both flawed and necessary.

It's flawed because some portion of returns are clearly taxed. Dividends are taxed. So is the profitable sale of stock. In the United States, short-term realized gains—from the sale of stock held one year or less—are taxed at the same high rate as ordinary income. Long-term capital gains are also taxed, though at lower federal rates.

It's necessary because tax rates vary greatly around the world. Even within a single country there are fully taxed, tax-deferred, and tax-free kinds of accounts. Plus some states and provinces tax, while others don't. In addition, an investor's total income from all sources can determine which tax rates apply. So it would be senseless to speak of *after-tax* returns when that means such different things to different people.

But that doesn't mean that tax doesn't matter. It does. It will emerge as significant later when we let it nudge us toward a strategy of picking stocks fit to hold for longer periods.

Sometimes one earmarks cash for stock investing, but fails to find a buying opportunity during a year. The amount was cash at the beginning of the year, cash during the year, and cash at the end of the year. It never found an equity home. As such it's excluded from the denominator. Should it be?

That depends what one wants to measure. If one wants to measure just the performance of a *fully invested* equity portfolio, then yes. Keep it out.

But if one wants to measure the total return from all assets under management earmarked for equity, then no. Add it. For consistency, also add any interest earned on that cash to the numerator.

Both approaches have merit. Excluding uninvested cash makes benchmarks more comparable. After all, indexes like the S&P 500 are fully invested by definition. They're all stocks. They have no cash.

But including uninvested cash can also make sense. It captures one's ability to *find* investments. We wouldn't want to fool ourselves into thinking that we didn't *try* to commit capital that we *couldn't*. Acknowledging that disappointment can provide encouragement for getting better at sourcing opportunities.

When I was a freshman at UCLA, I once met with the associate dean of housing. I was trying to hustle a prime dormitory room for my sophomore year. I failed. But the meeting was a success.

It was a success because, late in a wandering discussion about something else, this associate dean—thoughtful, nearing retirement, keen to hold forth—uttered this nugget:

*If you can identify it, you can manage it.*

I immediately knew that I'd heard something useful. In the three decades since that dry spring morning I have found that rule to be widely applicable.

It's particularly relevant to investing. When we correctly measure our investment performance, we *identify it*. Yes, calculating one's average return is exacting and bothersome. But it's no sideline. It's a prerequisite. It's a must if we're ever to *manage it*.

## Summary

Calculating one's own investment performance correctly involves three steps:

1. Measure the percentage return for each individual year.
2. Calculate the geometric average.
3. Compare the average to a standard.

# PART II

# THE VALUE INVESTING MODEL

## CHAPTER 5

# Understanding the Business

| Do I understand it? |
| --- |

Products
Customers
Industry
Form
Geography
Status

The value investing model begins with a fundamental question: do I understand it? The question stems from our recognition of stock as nothing less than *an ownership stake in a business.* So what we want to understand, specifically, is *the business.*

To understand a business is to be able to describe it in a single, unambiguous sentence. I call it an *understanding statement.* It's written in simple language that anyone can understand. Here's one for Wal-Mart:

*The company is the world's largest retailer, rushing value-priced merchandise like groceries to lower-income consumers through a chain of large stores located mostly in North America.*

The chance that whoever wrote this doesn't understand Wal-Mart is zero. There's a process used to formulate sentences like this. It involves defining the business along six parameters.

The first parameter is *products*. Are the company's products *goods* or *services*? That's an easy first distinction to draw. Goods are physical, and services are not. Samsung Electronics, the South Korean electronics manufacturer, sells goods. Southwest Airlines, the Dallas-based passenger airline, sells services.

Yes, Samsung also sells extended warranty contracts. Those are services. And Southwest also sells drinks, which are goods. But the bulk of each company's revenue clearly comes from goods and services respectively. Each company's 10-K makes that clear.

Another useful distinction is between *commodity* and *differentiated* products. A commodity has characteristics that can be objectively described on paper. A differentiated product is anything else.

Commodity and differentiated are at opposite ends of a spectrum on which all products lie. That is, there are greater and lesser grades of differentiation. The more important the brand is, the more differentiated the product is.

Take Horsehead Holdings, a Pittsburgh-based manufacturer of zinc.[1] Zinc is a metal used as a raw material in manufacturing. It's a commodity because it can be defined entirely on dimensions like weight, shape, and purity. That it bears the Horsehead brand name is unimportant.

By contrast, consider LVMH. It's the Paris-based producer of Louis Vuitton luggage and Thomas Pink shirts.[2] Its products are more differentiated. They're about look, feel, and associations. They don't lend themselves as readily to factual descriptions.

Good product definitions are narrow without being unnecessarily limiting. With Wal-Mart, *value-priced merchandise like groceries* is sufficient. It reflects the company's wide array of inexpensive wares, while highlighting groceries as its largest category.[3] In other cases the product definitions are less obvious.

Consider Vivint Solar, based in Utah. The company installs solar energy panels on houses, and leases these systems back to homeowners to yield lower overall energy costs. Its product might be called *residential solar energy services*.

But a thorough read of the company's 10-K reveals more. Vivint has a vice president of capital markets. It sponsors investment funds.[4] What is this, some kind of bank?

No, but Vivint does in fact offer a financial product. The solar systems that it deploys aren't owned by the company directly, but rather by partnerships that it establishes. Vivint recruits profitable American entities to invest in these partnerships. The arrangement entitles these entities to a special government credit—called a solar investment tax credit—that lowers the entity's taxable income. So yes, one of Vivint's products is residential solar energy services. But another is *tax credits*.

Why labor over product definitions? Because later on, we'll spend time identifying a company's competitive threats. If some day the United States Congress passes a bill offering tax credits for investments in, say, underground parking garages, that could decrease the investment dollars available for Vivint's funds. It would pose a threat. But if we failed to identify tax credits as a product, we'd miss that.

*Think plainly.* Unilever is the European producer of household brands like Dove shampoo, Knorr soup, and Lipton tea.[5] It would not be wrong to define Unilever's products as *fast-moving consumer goods*. Many do. But it's clearer to say *soap and food*.

The second parameter is *customers*. Customers buy a company's products. Are the customers *consumers* or *organizations*? Consumers are people buying for themselves or for their families. Organizations are governments, associations, and other businesses.

The more specific the customer definition, the better. Consider Chico's, a clothing store chain based in Florida.[6] It's correct to state that its customers are mostly women. But noting that its customers are middle-income women aged 35 or older is better. All that separates one from this level of detail is a thorough reading of Chico's 10-K, verified perhaps by a visit to one of its stores.

With Wal-Mart, *lower-income consumers* is as refined a customer definition as we need. This comes straight from the company's 10-K, which cites public assistance payments as a driver of its operating performance.[7] That line stands out. Nothing similar appears in the 10-K of the more midmarket Target chain, for example.[8]

Customers are different from *users*. I use Yahoo. But I've never paid Yahoo a nickel. Advertisers on Yahoo's websites, however, pay Yahoo plenty. They're the customers. The customers are the ones that pay the company.

A third parameter is *industry*. This is usually straightforward. Wal-Mart is clearly in *retailing*. But sometimes nuances appear.

Take Avon Products, the New York–based company associated with health and beauty. It's right to describe it as being in the cosmetics industry. But the company is among the largest direct-selling organizations in the world. It sells the *business opportunity* to sell cosmetics as an Avon independent representative.[9] In this way it's also in the *multilevel marketing* industry. Seeing this lets one identify other multilevel marketers dealing in different goods—like kitchen tools—as competitive.

A fourth parameter is *form*. Form is the way a business is structured, both legally and operationally.

The legal form of a business is usually unremarkable. Most public companies in the United States are *corporations*. If the name of an American business ends in *incorporated, inc, company, co, corporation*, or *corp*, it's a corporation. By the same token a *public limited company* in the United Kingdom ends in *PLC*, and an *aktiengesellschaft* in Germany ends in *AG*.

But sometimes a legal form is atypical. Noting this can help to explain what a business does. Consider Equity Residential, a Chicago-based owner of apartment buildings. Every year, Equity Residential pays out a big part of its net income to shareholders as dividends, bigger than that paid out by most listed American businesses. Why?

Because of its form. Equity Residential is structured as a real estate investment trust, or *REIT*.[10] REITs enjoy special tax benefits if they do certain things. For one, they have to get most of their income from real estate. Second, they have to pay out 90 percent of their taxable income as dividends. So the company pays enormous dividends *because it has to*. Recognizing Equity Residential's form is the key to grasping its dividend policy.

Form also refers to how a business is structured operationally. A company could be a *franchisor*, such as the Jack in the Box restaurant company based in San Diego. Or it could be a *franchisee* like Carrols Restaurant Group, which operates Burger Kings.

There are other operational structures. A company could be a *multilevel marketer* like Avon. Or it could be *vertically integrated*, operating along many nodes of its industry *value chain*.

SCA is a good example of a company with a vertically integrated operational form. The company is Europe's largest forest owner. It has timberland and sawmills, predictably. But it also owns several leading brands of diapers made out of the absorbent fluff pulp that it manufactures.[11] That a forest owner would make diapers—an activity normally done by separate companies that buy absorbent fluff pulp as a raw material—makes sense in the context of SCA's form.

Wal-Mart is organized such that it operates through subsidiaries and joint ventures. But that's normal. That's why our understanding statement doesn't say anything about the company's *legal* form. It's a plain corporation. But our understanding statement does sneak in a remark about its *operational* form. In saying that the company *rushes* products to consumers, it highlights the efficient internal distribution network that helps drive Wal-Mart's profitability.[12]

The fifth parameter is *geography*. Geography describes where the business's customers, operations, and headquarters are located, with the emphasis placed on whatever is most enlightening. Wal-Mart's most relevant geography concerns its stores. They're *located mostly in North America.*[13]

Geography can expose some thorny issues. Consider Philip Morris International, the cigarette manufacturer. It's headquartered in New York, and its stock trades on the New York Stock Exchange. But it sells exclusively in Asia, Africa, and elsewhere outside of America.[14] This liberates it from the cigarette sale and use restrictions of its home country and allows it to serve freer markets abroad. Since cigarettes are dangerous and addictive, one might see moral dimensions in this setup. Regardless, a grasp of this geographic reality is necessary to understand the business.

Sometimes the thorniness involves tax. Take Medtronic, the medical device manufacturer. The company started in the United States, where it continues to have operations. But after combining with smaller Dublin-based competitor Covidian, it's headquartered in Ireland.[15] Why?

Because of Ireland's lower corporate tax rates. Some see such tax-driven combinations—called *inversions*—as a way for companies to skirt obligations that they have to their original home countries. But whatever one's view, grasping the tax implications of geography is part of getting one's hands around a company.

The sixth parameter is *status*. This catchall category can be used for a company's prominence, age, transformation, or whatever else merits singling out.

Take Sears Holdings, the operator of department stores in the United States. A onetime retailing giant, the company by 2016 was unprofitable, losing revenue, and closing stores.[16] It's *fading.* The status parameter provides an opportunity to note this characteristic.

Other times the status parameter can be used to define a company's size. Our Wal-Mart understanding statement does this, calling it *the world's largest retailer.* Why is this relevant?

Because big successful companies can do things that small companies can't. They can raise capital on favorable terms, introduce new products with force, and absorb losses from new initiatives for years. They also have limitations. They have a hard time making changes unnoticed. They're easy targets for labor and environmental activists. And their histories tilt them toward defensive postures that keep them from adapting to market changes.

By the same token, small businesses have some advantages over large ones. They can pursue niche opportunities too small to interest bigger competitors. They can keep new product developments secret. And they're nimble enough to quickly meet new customer needs. These things are harder for Wal-Mart to do. Using the status parameter to call out Wal-Mart's bigness reveals an important set of both advantages and disadvantages.

Investing abounds in opportunities to complicate. Most people give in, proffering exhaustive descriptions that make much of minutiae. Resist. Think in straight lines. Defining the business along six parameters is a chance to seize clarity. Take it.

An old maxim in intelligent investing is to *buy what you know.*[17] This is solid advice, in theory. In practice, it is often applied too limitedly. People tend to mistake an understanding of *one* parameter with an understanding of *all six* parameters. They assume that if a part is in order, the whole is in order. This false assumption often centers on products.

Knowledge of a company's products is a common genesis of an investment idea. And it should be. A firsthand customer perspective is a good basis for analysis. But product understanding does not equal business understanding. It's a *component* of business understanding.

It can't substitute for the rounded view that objective definitions of all six parameters provide.

Product understanding, in other words, can be a *trap* when writing an understanding statement. It can masquerade as the whole picture. It's one of four traps to look out for.

A second trap is *marketing messages*. Also called *slogans*, they're designed to motivate customers. They're the stuff of advertisements. Wal-Mart's is "Save money. Live better."[18]

Marketing messages are an essential part of corporate communications. They can help the investor define a company's customers and products. But they should be recognized as the rallying cries that they are. They shouldn't be plugged unthinkingly into understanding statements.

The third trap is *mission statements*. Mission statements are marketing messages pointed inward. They highlight companies' goals and strengths, and are written to inspire employees, partners, and investors. Wal-Mart's is "We save people money so they can live better,"[19] an undisguised turn on its marketing message. Again, communications like this are important. But they're not ready-made modules of understanding statements.

The fourth trap is aspirations. Sometimes a company wants to have a characteristic that it presently does not. Take Clas Ohlson, a chain of hardware stores located principally in the Nordic countries of Sweden, Norway, and Finland. The company has made clear that is has designs on Germany, announcing plans to open three stores in Hamburg.[20] Should the company's store geography then be described as all of Northern Europe instead of just the Nordics?

No. Plans change, expansions falter, and the future generally turns out differently than forecast. It's not that a company articulating hopes is being deceptive or wrong. It's just that an understanding statement should focus on what a business *is* and not what it *could be*.

Some companies are composed of very different units. Each unit is a distinct company with its own products, customers, industry, form, geography, and status. When I encounter this, I do one of two things. If one unit constitutes the bulk of the company's activities, I define the six parameters for just that one. If the units are more equally weighted, I define all six separately for each.

Sometimes a business is sincerely difficult for me to understand. Its form may seem convoluted, its target market unclear, or its products puzzling. When this happens, one of two things is the case. First, the business may simply not be understandable by me. It may be just plain hard, or it may require a domain expertise that I lack.

The second possibility is that someone doesn't want me to understand it. Maybe a flawed business model is being deliberately obfuscated in the hopes that potential shareholders will mistake unintelligibility for flair.

Either way, I want no part of it. A investment idea that isn't understood can't move forward in the model.

The danger in investing in businesses that we don't understand isn't so much that we'll lose money. It's that we'll *make money*. Why? Because unless we're on our deathbed, this won't be our last trade. We'll naturally draw conclusions from an economic success that tilt us toward similar opportunities in the future. But if we never really understood the business, *we won't know what similar is*. Gains have a dangerous way of eclipsing this ignorance.

One concept that flows among value investors is *circle of competence*. It refers to the range of businesses that one is capable of understanding.[21] It's often used to justify *not* investing. Companies with highly technical products, or domiciled in developing countries with unclear regulations, are left unanalyzed because they're said to be *outside* one's circle of competence. Is this wise?

Maybe. But imagine freezing your circle of competence at age 12. What would you be capable of understanding today? Video game companies. Chocolate manufacturers. Maybe Disney. But General Electric?

Our circles of competence naturally evolve. Expertise we have in some fields atrophies, and in other fields grows. If we truly can't understand a business, we're right to look elsewhere. But if it just stretches us—if it *invites* us to learn something new—we should take advantage of that chance. We may discover something that—whether or not we invest in that particular company—expands the base of knowledge that we have to apply in the future. What seems fuzzy now may solidify later.

Soon we'll add more tools that help keep us from fooling ourselves into thinking that we understand a business that we don't. But just because one has to read up on a new subject doesn't mean that an idea is beyond reach. And even if it does turn out to be beyond reach, that doesn't mean that something constructive didn't happen. Proficiency accumulates.

## Summary

Define the business along six parameters:

1. Products
2. Customers
3. Industry
4. Form
5. Geography
6. Status

Don't be misled by:

1. Product familiarity
2. Marketing messages
3. Mission statements
4. Aspirations

# CHAPTER 6

# Accounting Is a Language

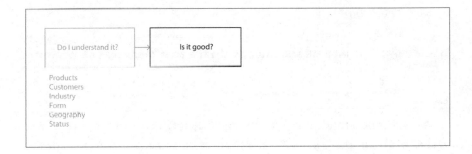

The second step in the model asks another fundamental question: Is it good? In other words, is the business worth owning at *some* price?

This question breaks into three subquestions. First, has the business been *historically* good? If so, is it likely to *remain* good in the future? And third, is it shareholder-friendly?

The first question—has it been historically good—is simple to answer. It's simple to answer because we have financial statements that report on how well the business did. We have a *record*.

Tackling financial statements requires fluency in the language of accounting. That's not hard to get. Cooking risotto is harder.

Even certified public accountants may find it useful to review the nature of financial statements from the simplistic perspective of the value investor.

A financial statement is a *quantitative description of a business*. Three financial statements matter: the *income statement*, the *cash flow statement*, and the *balance sheet*.

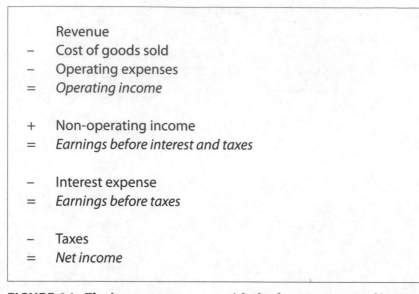

       Revenue
−    Cost of goods sold
−    Operating expenses
=    *Operating income*

\+    Non-operating income
=    *Earnings before interest and taxes*

−    Interest expense
=    *Earnings before taxes*

−    Taxes
=    *Net income*

**FIGURE 6.1:  The income statement with the four measures of income in *italics***

An income statement (Figure 6.1) describes a business over a period of time, like a year. It's sometimes called a *consolidated statement of operations*, a *profit and loss statement*, or simply a *P&L*.

The income statement first reports *revenue*. It's sales. Outside the United States it's sometimes called *turnover*.

An income statement next reports *cost of goods sold*. It's expenses that the business incurred to produce revenue.

The income statement then states *operating expenses*. They're costs recognized by the business *regardless of what was sold*. They're often called *selling, general and administrative expenses*, or *SG&A*. Outside the United States, operating expenses are sometimes presented in two separate lines: *selling expenses* and *administrative expenses*.

Operating expenses are different from cost of goods sold in that they're *not triggered by revenue*.

Finally, the income statement measures *income*. As we'll see, there are different measures of income. But generally speaking, *revenue minus cost of goods sold minus operating expenses equals income*.

Cash flow from operations
+ Cash flow from investments
+ Cash flow from financing
= Net cash flow

**FIGURE 6.2: The cash flow statement**

The second financial statement is the *cash flow statement* (Figure 6.2). Like the income statement, it describes a business over a period of time. It measures *cash flow*, which is the net amount of money entering or exiting a business. Cash flow is sometimes called *net cash flow*.

Cash *inflow* is cash coming *into* a business. Cash *outflow* is cash going *out* of a business. Cash inflow minus cash outflow equals net cash flow.

The cash flow statement sorts cash flows into three categories. Each category has its own cash inflows, cash outflows, and net cash flow.

The first category is *cash flow from operations*. It's the cash flow that results from the business *doing what it does*. Cash flow from operations is sometimes called *operating cash flow* or *cash flow from operating activities*.

Consider a wholesale beverage distributor. It buys bottled drinks for 50 cents each from a manufacturer and does nothing but sell the bottles to supermarkets for one dollar each. Its cash flow from operations would include the cash it receives from supermarkets, the cash it pays to manufacturers, and the cash it pays employees to receive, sort, and deliver bottles.

The second type of cash flow on a cash flow statement is *cash flow from investments*. It includes the purchase and sale of equipment that will last for multiple years. Such purchases are called *capital expenditures*. They appear on the cash flow statement as a cash outflow from investments called *purchase of property, plant, and equipment*.

Cash flow from investments is sometimes called *cash flow from investing activities*.

Think again about the wholesale beverage distributor. If it paid $500,000 in cash to buy a warehouse, then cash flow from investments would go down by $500,000. If it sold one of its delivery trucks for $10,000, cash flow from investments would go up by $10,000.

The third category of cash flow is *cash flow from financing*. A company borrowing money from a bank, or selling half of itself to investors for cash, are examples of cash inflows from financing. A company paying the bank back, or buying back its own shares, are examples of cash outflows from financing.

Cash flow from financing is sometimes called *cash flow from financing activities*.

Cash flow statements can be prepared by either the *direct method* or the *indirect method*. The difference is only in the top third of the cash flow statement, *cash flow from operations*.

The direct method is simpler. Under it, the section begins with cash inflows from operations, proceeds to cash outflows from operations, and ends with net cash flow from operations.

Under the indirect method, the section begins with the net income line from the income statement. It then adds and subtracts various things to yield the ending net cash flow from operations line. It's convoluted. But most listed companies use the indirect method.

The main difference between the cash flow statement and the income statement is that the cash flow statement uses the *cash basis* of accounting, and the income statement uses the *accrual basis* of accounting.

The cash basis is stupider. It's like a turnstile. It just watches money flow in and out the business. The only clever thing it does is sort the money into one of three categories.

The accrual basis is smarter. It's like a doorman. It makes judgments. It decides things like how much revenue should be booked based on inventory shipped, how much cost of goods sold was incurred based on inventory purchase prices, and how much operating expense to recognize based on employee working hours.

Both the income statement and the cash flow statement look at a business over a period of time. They're like *movies*.

The third financial statement is the *balance sheet* (Figure 6.3). It looks at a business at a *single point* in time. It's not like a movie. It's like a *snapshot*.

```
Assets      =      Liabilities
                 +   Equity
```

**FIGURE 6.3:  The balance sheet**

The balance sheet shows what a business *owns*, what a business *owes*, and the *difference between the two*.

What a business owns is called *assets*. What a business owes is called *liabilities*. And the difference between the two is called *equity*. If a business has more liabilities than assets, it has *negative equity*.

Assets are things that a business *controls*, *finds valuable*, and *bought*. There are two kinds of assets: *current assets* and *noncurrent assets*. Cash is a current asset. Any asset that could be used within a year is also a current asset.

Consider again the wholesale beverage distributor. Bottled drinks that it buys from a manufacturer but has not yet delivered to supermarkets are current assets. Specifically, the bottled drinks are a type of current asset called *inventory*. Inventory is also called *stock-in-trade*.

Noncurrent assets generally take more than a year to use. A delivery truck owned by the wholesale beverage distributor is a noncurrent asset.

Assume that the distributor buys a new truck for $30,000 in cash. On the cash flow statement, cash flow from investments decreases by $30,000, and net cash flow decreases by $30,000. On the balance sheet, current assets decrease by $30,000; and noncurrent assets increase by $30,000.

Assume that the truck will last for three years. After three years, it will be worthless. In other words, the distributor will "use" one-third of the truck's price each year. How is this accounted for?

Each year, the distributor will decrease the *book value* of the truck by $10,000 on the balance sheet. It will do this by recognizing a $10,000 operating expense on the income statement. This process of decreasing the book value of a noncurrent asset by recognizing an expense on the income statement is called *depreciation*.

If the noncurrent asset is *intangible*, the same process is called *amortization*. Examples of intangible noncurrent assets are patents and trademarks.

If a noncurrent tangible asset does not lose value over time, it is not depreciated. Land is the best example of a noncurrent tangible asset that is not depreciated.

The purchase of a noncurrent asset is the same as a capital expenditure.

Sometimes a business buys an asset that will last for many years, but the business does not *capitalize* the asset. That is, the business recognizes the full price as an operating expense on the income statement at the time of purchase. This happens when the price of the asset is small. For example, an $8 pencil sharpener may last for many years, but because $8 is small, the business will expense it all immediately. In other words, the price is not *material*.

Another way to think about it is that because the pencil sharpener fails a materiality test, it is *depreciated all at once*.

The second section on the balance sheet is *liabilities*. Money borrowed from a bank is a liability, because it must be paid back. If the distributor receives a delivery of bottled drinks from the manufacturer and has not yet paid for it, the money that the distributor owes to the manufacturer is a liability. Specifically, it's a type of liability called an *account payable*.

The third section on the balance sheet is equity. Equity is sometimes called *shareholders' equity*, *owners' equity*, *net assets*, or *book value*. Equity equals assets minus liabilities.

After assets, liabilities, and equity, the balance sheet has a final line called *liabilities and equity*. This line provides no new information. It just proves that liabilities plus equity equals assets. Sometimes the line is called *total liabilities and shareholders' equity*.

Consider again intangible assets. In addition to patents and trademarks, there's another sort of intangible asset called *goodwill*.

Goodwill is easy to understand. Assume that the balance sheet equity of company B is $1,000,000. Company A acquires company B for $1,500,000 in cash. Immediately after the acquisition, company A increases the goodwill on its balance sheet by $500,000. That is, goodwill equals *acquisition price in excess of equity*.

The order of the sections on the balance sheet vary. In the United States, liabilities are presented before equity. The reverse is sometimes true elsewhere. But the substance of the balance sheet, and of its sections, is the same.

Generally, a business is said to *make money* if it shows positive income on its income statement. If this income is *retained*—that is, not paid out as *dividends*—then equity increases by that amount. Income that is kept in the business is called *retained earnings*.

American financial statements are prepared in accordance with US GAAP, or U.S. generally accepted accounting principles. It's a set of guidelines. In much of the rest of the world, they're prepared in accordance with IFRS, international financial reporting standards. This difference doesn't obstruct the value investor. But there are some contrasts.

For example, one type of cash outflow is interest payments. Under US GAAP, interest payments appear on the cash flow statement in the *cash flow from operations* section. But under IFRS, interest payments could appear in either that or the *cash flow from financing* section.[1] Later on this difference will turn out to be important. But like all other differences between US GAAP and IFRS, it's masterable.

The interest payment example highlights an oddity. What's an interest payment? It's a fee paid for borrowing money. Sometimes it's paid to a bank. Other times it's paid to a bondholder. Either way, it's paid to some entity that extended a loan to the company.

That loan, of course, is part of the company's *capital structure*. It's part of the financial base of the business. So an interest payment happens because of a financing decision. Therefore, it feels like a cash outflow from *financing*. It is after all a cash outflow, and it occurs only because of a financing. Then why under US GAAP are interest payments classed as cash outflows from *operations*?

There's no great answer. Sometimes companies pay bills late, and vendors may charge an interest penalty as a result. Such charges may feel like bona fide cash outflows from operations, since they originate with normal purchases. But these kinds of interest payments are often tiny compared to interest paid on outstanding financial debt. Why then does US GAAP have this rule? To understand, consider an analogy.

In the English language, adjectives go before nouns. If you were going to visit a friend in England who lived in a white house, you might ask for directions to just that: a *white house*. But if you were visiting a friend in Spain, you'd do the opposite. You'd put the adjective *after* the noun. You'd be looking for a *casa blanca*.

Is Spanish *wrong*?

No, of course not. It's just that a convention of the Spanish language is to put nouns before adjectives. It's a *standard*. It would be meaningless, in other words, to cite Spanish for violating some divine law of communication.

The same is true of accounting. It's just a set of standards. Much of the frustration with accounting comes from demanding that it square with some sort of celestial bookkeeping truth. But there's no such thing.

Of course accounting isn't *random*. Depreciation does, for example, reflect the fact that some things do really wear out over time. But accounting isn't humankind's watertight solution to measuring commercial reality. It's just a set of rules that people have agreed to use to describe businesses in numbers.

This may feel unsatisfying. That accounting should be more fiat than science can seem downright *empty*. But just as asking for directions to a *blanca casa* may get one lost in Madrid, insisting that accounting mesh with some greater logic can tie one up needlessly.

Give in. Accept accounting as the quirky language that it is, and bite into the infinitely more interesting matters that value investing offers.

## Summary

Value investors must master three financial statements:

1. Income statement
2. Cash flow statement
3. Balance sheet

## CASE STUDY

## LinkedIn Corporation

LinkedIn is a career-oriented social network based near San Francisco. First publicly traded in 2011, the company's 2015 10-K presents representatively complex financial statements. A walk through the income statement, cash flow statement, and balance sheet show how the important concepts of accounting can be made to jump out:

> http://www.goodstockscheap.com/6.1.htm

LinkedIn's income statement is on page 73. It's called the *consolidated statement of operations*, a common synonym for income statement. *Consolidated* means that results from any LinkedIn subsidiaries are included. That's normal.

The income statement's first line is *net revenue*, which is the same as *revenue* or *turnover*. It was $2,990,911,000 in 2015.

Of course the revenue number that appears is 1/1,000th of that. But the income statement's heading says that all numbers are in thousands. So we add three zeroes.

The *net* in *net revenue* means two things. First is the exclusion of sales tax, since that's quickly turned over to government agencies. It's just *passing through* the company, like a traveler changing planes. Second is an estimate of refunds that the company may pay out in the future. This is all spelled out in the *notes to consolidated financial statements* on page 81.

*Cost of goods sold* is also identified by a synonym: *cost of revenue (exclusive of depreciation and amortization shown separately below).* Why the bit in parentheses? After all, depreciation and amortization are commonly part of *operating expenses*. They're *often* absent from cost of goods sold.

Extra qualifiers like this often appear. Roll with them. They're harmless. In any case, the company's cost of goods sold for 2015 was $418,858,000.

*Operating expenses* is not stated so clearly. It's split among four expense lines: *sales and marketing*, *product development*, *general and administrative*, and *depreciation and amortization*. By their names alone, these are obviously operating expenses as opposed to cost of goods sold. They're the sorts of expenses that happen regardless of what was sold during any single period. For 2015, they add up to $2,722,995,000.

That a company wouldn't give its operating expenses in one clean line isn't shocking. Financial statements *never* lay out exactly as anticipated. Abnormalities are normal. Handling this is as easy as being ready for it.

Subtracting cost of goods sold and operating expenses from revenue yields ($150,942,000). The parentheses mean negative. This is the first measure of income: *operating income*. LinkedIn calls it *income (loss) from operations*, an easily identified equivalent. It's just $2,990,911,000 minus $418,858,000 minus $2,722,995,000.

Sometimes an income statement then shows another line called *non-operating income*. It's gains or losses from noncore activities, like foreign exchange. Operating income plus non-operating income yields a second measure of income: *earnings before interest and taxes*, or *EBIT*.

LinkedIn happens not to state non-operating income in one clean line. But there is a section called *other income (expense), net* that contains three lines. Two of them sound to me like non-operating income. One is *interest income*. It's $10,571,000. Another is *other, net*. It's ($23,477,000). So LinkedIn's EBIT equals ($163,848,000). That's just ($150,942,000) plus $10,571,000 plus ($23,477,000).

The other line in that section is *interest expense*. For 2015 it's ($50,882,000). Subtracting interest expense from EBIT gives a third measure of income, *earnings before taxes*. That's ($163,848,000) plus ($50,882,000), which equals ($214,730,000).

There's one final expense line on the income statement: *taxes*. LinkedIn calls it *provision (benefit) for income taxes*. In 2015 it was ($49,969,000). That's a *negative expense*.

In other words, the company recognized some sort of tax *benefit* in 2015. Subtracting this from earnings before taxes yields the final measure of income: *net income*. LinkedIn calls it *net income (loss) attributable to common stockholders*. It was ($164,761,000) in 2015. That is, the company *lost* $164,761,000.

The cash flow statement, on page 76, is similarly masterable. LinkedIn calls it the *consolidated statements of cash flows*.

The first thing to notice is that it was prepared by the *indirect method*. This is obvious from the organization of the first section, *operating activities*. It starts with net income, and then makes a series of adjustments to reach what it calls *net cash provided by operating activities*. This is the same as *net cash flow from operations*. In 2015 it was $806,975,000.

The second section of the cash flow statement, *investing activities*, starts with the line *purchases of property and equipment*. That's the same as *capital expenditures*. It's given as ($507,246,000) for 2015. Note again the parentheses, implying minus. Since that line regards purchases, is this a double negative? Did the company *receive* $507,246,000?

No. But this highlights a bizarre convention of accounting: the presentation of negative numbers in a section already understood to be about outflows or costs. The opposite—an outflow or costs section *without* parentheses—also happens, and also without explanation. No standard seems to exist. But again, managing this inconsistency is as straightforward as anticipating it.

The second section ends with the line *net cash used in investing activities*, which is the same as *net cash flow from investing activities*. For 2015, it's ($792,077,000). In other words, LinkedIn had a net cash outflow of $792,077,000 from its investing activities in 2015.

The balance sheet is on page 72. *Assets*—called *total assets*—equals $7,011,199,000. Next is *liabilities*. LinkedIn calls it *total liabilities*. It's $2,515,746,000. We'd therefore expect *equity* to be $4,495,453,000, since that's assets minus liabilities. But the line called *total stockholders' equity* gives a smaller number: $4,468,643,000. Why?

Well, the difference between the figure on the balance sheet and what was expected is ($26,810,000). That's the same number given for something on the balance sheet called *redeemable noncontrolling interest*. What's that?

The 10-K doesn't say. But it doesn't have to. One just needs to note that that amount *reduces* equity.

As we'll see later, equity is a good thing. The higher it is, the better a company looks. But the astute investor views potential buys conservatively. By that principal alone, the smaller equity figure of $4,468,643,000 is more useful.[2]

The redeemable noncontrolling interest turns out to be discussed in the *prior* year's 10-K. It's the portion of LinkedIn's China operation that's owned by a minority partner.[3] It's something that a shareholder in LinkedIn wouldn't own.

LinkedIn's financial statements aren't the easiest to read. They require interpretation, calculations, and assumptions.

But it's always like that. Companies present themselves differently. Even within the same country, the same industry, and the same year, there are variances. Expect them. Welcome them, even, because one's fluency in accounting is built on the test of a thousand twists. Facility develops with each financial statement read until the unexpected dissolves into readiness.

## CHAPTER 7

# Capital Employed

Fluency in accounting lets one make financial statements talk. Specifically, one can make them cough up six *key numbers*. The numbers can then be used to calculate *performance metrics*. These performance metrics make clear whether or not a business has been *historically good*.

One key number is *capital employed*. Capital employed is a company's *required financial base*. It's the resources that have to be there in order for the company to maintain its level of operations.

I've driven south from Palo Alto to Santa Barbara many times. Fifty, maybe. And at some point during each trip I start to wonder: where does *Southern* California begin?

There's no border. Northern and Southern California are loosely defined parts of the same state. So the answer is open to interpretation.

Some say San Luis Obispo, because that's where the smells start to change from farm to ocean. Others say Santa Barbara itself, because that's where beach volleyball becomes more popular than mountain biking. Some extremists suggest that Palo Alto is actually *in* Southern California because from there it's still 400 miles north to the Oregon border. The definition is always subjective, yet to each person, obvious.

Capital employed is like that. Each value investor has a definition that is subjective, yet firmly held. But a particular interpretation matters less than the fact that one is considering it at all. Few brokerage account holders have ever even *heard* of capital employed. Estimating it kicks off an analytical process that confers advantage.

I measure capital employed by starting with *total assets* and then subtracting *excess cash* and *non-interest-bearing current liabilities*. These figures come from the balance sheet.

Picture the start of a basic bicycle rental business. Absurdly basic: the rental of a single bicycle. Assume that the bike costs $1,000, and that there are no other start-up costs. The amount of capital that must be invested in the business, then, is $1,000. Once the bike is purchased, the rentals can begin.

That $1,000 has to *stay* in the business. If the $1,000—now incarnated as the bicycle—disappears, the renting stops. There'd be nothing left to rent out. So $1,000 is the business's capital employed at inception.

Note that the *type* of financing doesn't matter. It could be debt, or it could be equity. If the business borrowed the $1,000, capital employed is $1,000. If the business raised the $1,000 by selling new stock in itself, capital employed is still $1,000. Capital employed is blind to the *type* of finance.

Now assume that $1,000 *wasn't* the amount initially raised. Instead, it was $1,500. Everything else is the same. The bicycle is purchased for $1,000, and the rentals commence at the same scale as in the earlier example. The extra $500 just sits there.

This $500 is *excess*. It doesn't have to stay in the business. So it's *not* part of capital employed. It's capital, but it's not *employed*. Ideally, one would subtract it.

The trouble is that spotting excess cash is awfully difficult. Imagine receiving the bike rental venture's balance sheet. Would the $500 jump out as excess? Perhaps, if one assumed that *any* cash was excess cash. If the cash really needed to be there, one could reason, it would already have been used to *buy* something.

But how could one be sure that the $500 wouldn't be needed *tomorrow*? What if a tire pops?

It gets trickier. Imagine that the $500 didn't just sit there, but was rather used to buy a *centrifuge*. That is, something *totally unrelated* to the bike rental business. The centrifuge seems just as excess as idle cash. Perhaps what one should really deduct is not just excess cash, but all excess *assets*. But determining which assets are unnecessary just by looking at a balance sheet is hard.

Scale these issues up to the level of a big listed company, and it's easy to see how imprecise things can get. How much cash does a business really need?

One popular way to answer this question is to assume that a set percentage of revenue equals the amount of required cash. Each fan of this approach seems to have a favorite percentage, one applied to all kinds of businesses. Five percent, for example. By this logic a company with $1,000,000,000 in annual revenue and a cash balance of $100,000,000 would have excess cash of $50,000,000.

That's ridiculous. It's a fine example of finance's embrace of formulas in a desperate claw for certainty.

Different businesses are *different*. How much cash a firm needs to have on hand depends on its business model, how fast customers pay, and how fast vendors need to be paid. Applying the same percent every time is like always using a spoon regardless of what's for lunch.

Not that there's a perfect solution. But absent any specific guidance, one approach is to calculate two versions of capital employed: one with *all* cash subtracted, and one with *no* cash subtracted. When we later calculate performance metrics, it will be clear how practical this is.

My formula for capital employed also calls for the subtraction of *non-interest-bearing current liabilities*. This includes *accounts payable*, *deferred income*, and *accrued expenses*. These quantities are often broken out clearly on the balance sheet.

Accounts payable is money owed to vendors. Deferred income is advance payments received for products not yet delivered to customers. And accrued expenses are periodic amounts owed but not yet paid, like salaries. Note that these are all debts that will be squared *soon*. They'd better not have to stay in the business, because they're *leaving*.

Why the *non-interest-bearing* bit? To keep financial debt *in* the calculation of capital employed. When a company borrows money, it often does so for terms longer than a year. On the balance sheet, such loans are categorized as *noncurrent liabilities*, sometimes called *long-term liabilities*. As such, this debt would naturally wind up in the calculation of capital employed.

But as these loans come due, they slip into the *current liabilities* section. The fundamental nature of the obligations hasn't changed, but the passage of time has forced them into another category. They must now be paid back soon. Because they're loans, the company pays interest on them. So the non-interest-bearing stipulation makes it clear that they belong *in* capital employed.

Some investors subtract not only *excess cash* and *non-interest-bearing current liabilities* from total assets, but also *goodwill*. Recall that when a company makes an acquisition, the amount paid in excess of book value is goodwill. Is this part of capital employed?

That depends. Consider Cisco Systems, the networking equipment company based near San Francisco. The company made 8 acquisitions in 2014,[1] 13 the year before,[2] and 7 the year before that.[3] Acquisitions are clearly *part of what it does*.

The company's goodwill increased by $2.3 billion in 2014 and constituted almost a quarter of its total assets by the end of that year.[4] At Cisco, goodwill feels almost as ongoing and significant as capital expenditures. Obviously, money raised to finance capital expenditures belongs in capital employed. Perhaps goodwill does too.

The astute investor makes a judgment in deciding whether or not to deduct goodwill. To me, the key issue is how recurring the increases in goodwill are. The more frequently a company makes acquisitions, the less deducting goodwill makes sense. I often leave it in.

My capital employed formula has a specific view behind it: *all assets in the business need to be in the business unless proven otherwise*. I start with a huge number—total assets—and chip away at it selectively. Only those items that certainly aren't required get subtracted.

Sometimes calculating capital employed also requires *adding* some items. This happens when the company has liabilities not represented on the balance sheet. They're real obligations, but they escape accounting recognition.

Think again about the bicycle rental business. Assume that all of its $1,000 in start-up capital was *borrowed*. It's all *debt*. And it's all used to buy the bicycle. On day one the bank account is empty, the bicycle stands ready for rental, and capital employed is $1,000.

Now imagine a different beginning. Picture the business not buying the bicycle, but rather *leasing* it. No money needs to be raised—debt or otherwise—because $1,000 isn't needed to start the venture. Instead, the business agrees to lease the bicycle from its owner—a leasing company—for 10 years. At the end of each year the business will pay the leasing company a predetermined lease fee out of the rents received from customers. On day one the bank account is empty, the bicycle stands ready for rental, and capital employed is *zero*.

In both cases, the business assumed an obligation. But only in the first—the debt case—is the obligation recognized as capital employed. In the second it looks initially like the business doesn't need *any* financial base. An adjustment can fix that misrepresentation.

Accounting sees two kinds of leases. One is called an *operating lease*. It's what our bicycle example envisions. Lease expenses are recognized on the income statement when they're due. Cash outflows from operations are recognized on the cash flow statement when they're paid. But that's it. Nothing shows up on the balance sheet. For this reason, an operating lease is said to be *off balance sheet*.

The second kind of lease accounting sees is called a *capital lease*. The company reports as if it had purchased the equipment, and had borrowed money to do so. It's *on balance sheet*. It sees the lease as a debt every bit as real as money owed to a lender.

A capital lease drags leased equipment onto the balance sheet. It increases liabilities and assets by an equivalent amount. This forces leased equipment into any measurement of capital employed, since it's now part of total assets.

US GAAP has rules for determining when a lease is accounted for as the operating or capital sort. If the lessee assumes most of the risks of owning the equipment, and enjoys most of the benefits, then it's a capital lease. Specifically, it's a capital lease if one of four conditions holds: ownership transfers to the lessee at the end of the lease term, the lessee has the option to purchase the equipment inexpensively, the lease term equals at least three-fourths of the equipment's estimated useful life, or the minimum lease payments have a *present value* of at least nine-tenths of the fair value of the equipment.

If only one of these four conditions holds, then the equipment naturally winds up in the calculation of capital employed.

IFRS doesn't provide as rigid a test, but it does say something similar. It says that if substantially all the risks and rewards of ownership go to the lessee, then it's a capital lease. In many countries outside of the United States where IFRS is used, a capital lease is called a *finance lease.*

The challenge comes when *accounting standards* see an operating lease, but the *investor* smells a capital lease. The solution is to adjust capital employed upward by *capitalizing the operating lease.*

Capitalizing operating leases is like squeezing your own orange juice. It's a lot of work for what you get. But it's a skill worth mastering. Many good investors insist that *all* operating leases should be capitalized. One shouldn't fear reaching that conclusion just because implementing it is knotty. We'll unknot it shortly. But first, it's worth reviewing a term used earlier: *present value.*

To a company that owes a debt, a dollar owed in a year is worth more than a dollar owed today. There are two ways to see this. First, a dollar owed in a year can be invested for a 12-month period that the dollar leaving today doesn't have. Just depositing the dollar in the bank, for example, will yield *something.*

Second, inflation acts to make the dollar paid in a year *less valuable* than the dollar paid today. Its purchasing power will drop over time, as did my $1.25 in Balboa Bar money from 1979. Later, the dollar will be less painful to part with.

These two truths underpin the concept of present value. The present value of an amount of money owed in the future is that amount *discounted back to now* at some rate. It's a quantitative estimate.

For example, $100 slated to be paid exactly one year from now would have a present value of $90.91 if discounted back at the rate of 10 percent. Spreadsheets make this easy to see. Microsoft Excel, Google Sheets, and Apache OpenOffice all have a built-in function called NPV. Plugging the $100 nominal amount and 10 percent rate into the NPV function yields the $90.91 present value.

Where did the 10 percent discount rate come from? Nowhere special. In the context of a capitalized operating lease, it's meant to equal the interest rate at which the company could borrow money to buy the equipment. As we'll see, 10-Ks provide clues useful in its estimation. But it's just a guess.

Nailing down exact discount rates is the subject of much fussiness. It's a good example of precision masquerading as accuracy.

I prefer a straightforward approach that aborts any illusion of certainty. Jumping ahead briefly, if an investment opportunity looks good at one discount rate but miserable at one 100 basis points away, it's not much of an opportunity. Great buys have a way of shining through all kinds of assumptions.

Present value is important in the capitalization of operating leases because it determines how much of a liability, and corresponding asset, is added to the balance sheet.

When an operating lease is capitalized, all three financial statements change. Specifically, six things happen. Each of them makes sense when one remembers that the point is to pretend that equipment that was *leased* was instead *bought with borrowed money*.

First, the lease expense is added back on the income statement. Second, the lease payments are added back on the cash flow statement. Third, a liability is added to the balance sheet, as is an equivalent asset. Fourth, interest is expensed on the income statement. Fifth, interest payments are outflowed on the cash flow statement. Sixth, the lease asset is depreciated on the income statement.

This sketch of all six steps helps one appreciate what capitalizing an operating lease means. We'll flesh out each step later. But for now, note that the only one initially relevant to capital employed is the third. That's the one that fluffs the balance sheet up to its true size.

The amount of the liability added to the balance sheet, and the corresponding asset, is the present value of the future expenses under the lease. Calculating it requires two things: the future lease expenses and a discount rate.

In a 10-K the future lease expenses appear in a table following the financial statements. Search for the term *non-cancelable* or *lease payments*. The table lays out the lease expenses scheduled for each of the next five years, plus a sixth amount equal to the sum of all lease expenses scheduled from year six through the year in which the last lease expires. One must make a rough guess to allocate this sixth amount among the last set of years.

The discount rate is the percentage the company pays to borrow money. A 10-K often reveals the company's most recent cost of debt, expressed as an interest rate. This is the percentage to use. Search for the terms *long-term debt*, *interest rate*, or *senior note*. The higher the discount rate, the smaller the present value.

The logic behind capitalizing leases lies in seeing the equipment owner as both a *vendor* and a *lender*. It's a vendor in that it supplies the equipment. But it's also a lender in that it *borrowed money on the business's behalf* to buy the equipment. Put differently, capital leases *look through* leasing companies.

Big companies lease different kinds of assets. Equipment is one. For example, airlines commonly enter into operating leases for aircraft. Real estate is another. It's common for retailers to work with landlords to design contracts that *barely* permit operating lease accounting. Whatever the asset, operating leases can mask the full scope of a company's liabilities.

Besides capitalizing operating leases, there are other gymnastics one could perform to better calculate capital employed. For example, one could further fluff up the balance sheet by adjusting for unfunded pension plans. But there's a point at which the cost of further analysis outweighs the likelihood of a better decision. Identifying that point well gets easier with experience.

Capital employed is only one way to conceptualize a company's required financial base. Another is *invested capital*. By some formulas, it's equivalent to capital employed. But the thinking behind it is different.

Invested capital is the total amount of money committed to a company by *parties that expect a financial return*. Shareholders expect a financial return. So do bondholders. But vendors—like landlords that just want to get paid—don't. They're not expecting interest, dividends, appreciation, or anything else besides their rent. They wouldn't think of themselves as *investors* in the company in the way that shareholders and noteholders would.

The invested capital notion of a company's required financial base suggests different math. It suggests adding up all the capital that has been contributed by parties that expect a financial return. Equity plus financial debt, basically.

But this *additive* method may lack a benefit of the *subtractive* method used to calculate capital employed. Starting with total assets and deducting only those things that clearly don't belong reduces the chance of *underestimating* a company's required financial base. As we'll see when we start calculating metrics, this lessens the risk that one will see diamonds where there is only glass.

## Summary

1. Capital employed is one measure of a company's required financial base.
2. Capital employed is total assets minus excess cash minus non-interest-bearing current liabilities, and possibly minus goodwill.
3. Total assets can include capitalized operating leases.
4. Capitalizing operating leases causes all three financial statements to change.
5. Considering a company's required financial base is more important than measuring it perfectly.

**CASE STUDY**

## The Gap, Inc.

Gap is an American chain of clothing stores. Its 2015 10-K offers representative challenges in estimating capital employed:

http://www.goodstockscheap.com/7.1.htm

The balance sheet is on page 34. The first number to find is *total assets*. On January 30, 2016—the last day of fiscal year 2015—it's given as $7,473,000,000.

The next number to identify is cash. Gap's balance sheet uses the common synonym *cash and cash equivalents. Cash equivalents* are high-quality securities that can become cash within three months.

U.S. government treasury bills, for example. They're as good as cash for our purposes. In any case, the total was $1,370,000,000 at the end of fiscal 2015.

How much of this cash is excess? Over a billion dollars sounds like a lot. But as usual, it's hard to tell. So this number will later be used to calculate two versions of capital employed: one with all cash subtracted, and one with no cash subtracted.

The next step is to sort through the current liabilities section to see which should be subtracted. The section contains four lines. The first is *current maturities of debt*. The words *maturities* and *debt* both imply an interest-bearing liability. This is an amount owed to lenders. What's in it was probably in the *long-term liabilities* section of *last* year's balance sheet. Then as now, it was part of the capital structure of the company. So it stays.

Second is *accounts payable*, the perfect example of a non-interest-bearing current liability. It's $1,112,000,000. It gets subtracted.

Next is *accrued expenses and other current liabilities*. What does *other* mean? There's no footnote offering a description. But a search for the term *accrued expenses and other current liabilities* helps. The eighth appearance of these words is as the title of a table that breaks the whole amount into four components. It's on page 48.

The first component is *unredeemed gift cards, gift certificates, and credit vouchers, net of breakage*. I know people that get Gap gift cards for their birthday and *never* redeem them. So maybe that amount is not all about to get settled. I don't subtract it.

The next component is *accrued compensation and benefits*. This sounds like amounts owed to employees between pay periods, so it gets subtracted. It's $230,000,000.

Next is *short-term deferred rent and tenant allowances*. This is obviously some real estate related liability. It's not clear that it won't be there next year. So it stays.

The fourth component, *other*, is nebulous. If the burden of proof rests with the item to warrant subtraction—as I think it does—then it stays.

The fourth and final line in the current liabilities section of the balance sheet is *income taxes payable*. It's $23,000,000. Should this be subtracted?

How much tax is owed is a regular topic of discussion between a big company and its taxing authorities. It can go unresolved for years. As such, government can be viewed as a kind of lender that extends credit in the form of temporary tax relief, much as a bank extends credit in the form of a loan. For this reason an income tax liability could be considered part of a company's capital base, and not subtracted in the calculation of capital employed.

But there's something about the word *payable* that suggests *final*. It sounds like the discussion is over, and a known amount is about to get paid. Therefore, the $23,000,000 goes.

One may decide to simply deduct all *non-interest-bearing current liabilities* without scrutiny. That should work acceptably. I prefer a closer look both to lessen the chance that I'll underestimate the required financial base and because it may help me to better understand the business.

It's now possible to take a first stab at Gap's capital employed. It's *total assets* of $7,473,000,000, minus *accounts payable* of $1,112,000,000, minus *accrued compensation and benefits* of $230,000,000, minus *income taxes payable* of $23,000,000. So including cash, capital employed is $6,108,000,000.

Subtracting cash of $1,370,000,000 from this number yields $4,738,000,000. That's capital employed assuming that Gap needs *none* of its cash.

As a retailer, Gap could have a lot of operating leases. A search for the term *capital lease* turns up nothing. But the term *operating lease* gets seven hits. The most useful is note 11 on page 61. It begins, "We lease most of our store premises and some of our corporate facilities and distribution centers. These operating leases. . . ."

So *all* of the company's leases are accounted for as operating leases. *None* are capitalized.

Note 11 makes capitalizing Gap's operating leases simple. It says that the scheduled lease expenses are $1,135,000,000 in 2016, $1,098,000,000 in 2017, $946,000,000 in 2018, $821,000,000 in 2019, and $682,000,000 in 2020. Enter each year and its corresponding expense into a two-row spreadsheet.

The note then says that Gap will incur total lease expenses of $2,118,000,000 between 2021 and 2032. That's a 12-year period.

Dividing $2,118,000,000 by 12 yields $176,500,000. That's one way to allocate the amount among the remaining years: evenly.

But note that the annual lease expense gradually declines between 2016 and 2020. Perhaps a better approach is to extend this trend. Try expensing $500,000,000 in 2021, $400,000,000 in 2022, $300,000,000 in 2023 and $200,000,000 in 2024.

The original $2,118,000,000 minus these four amounts equals $718,000,000. That's a relatively small number, so allocating it evenly among the eight remaining years seems sensible. Dividing $718,000,000 by eight yields $89,750,000. Use this estimate for each year starting with 2025 and ending with 2032.

Add all of the 2021 through 2032 figures to the spreadsheet.

Incidentally, the declining lease expenses between 2016 and 2020 doesn't mean that Gap is shrinking. These are just the lease expenses that the company had already committed to at the end of fiscal year 2015. There's still plenty of time for Gap to sign new leases for those later years.

To pick a discount rate, search for the term *long-term debt*. The ninth hit is note 4 on page 50. It details three borrowings. The first is a $1,250,000,000 note that matures in April of 2021. Gap is apparently paying 5.95 percent interest for this money. That would do for a discount rate, except that a quick Internet search shows that that note was issued way back in April 2011.[5] Interest rates have dropped since then, making this reference point stale.

The next candidate is a 15 billion Japanese yen loan that Gap took out in January 2014. The interest rate fluctuates, but in 2015 it was apparently 1 percent. This data point is more current. But most of the property that Gap leases is in America. It would have to be purchased with U.S. dollars, not Japanese yen. So there might be some foreign exchange cost not captured in the 1 percent interest rate.

The last reference point is a $400,000,000 loan that Gap took out in October 2015. It also seems to float around 1 percent. Unfortunately the loan matures in October 2016, making it too short-term a debt to be comparable to that which Gap would take on to buy real estate.

So there's no perfect reference point. *But there never is.* My opinion is that 4 percent—a rate somewhere between that of the April 2021 note and the Japanese yen loan—suffices.

Discounting the 17-year stream of lease expenses at a 4 percent discount rate yields $5,693,244,523. This is the amount to add to both liabilities and assets:

> http://www.goodstockscheap.com/7.2.xlsx

This makes Gap's capital employed with cash equal to $11,801,244,523. That's just $6,108,000,000—the old figure for capital employed with cash—plus the capitalized operating leases' present value of $5,693,244,523.

Without cash, capital employed is $10,431,244,523. That's $4,738,000,000—the old figure for capital employed *without* cash— plus the same capitalized operating leases' present value.

Note the enormous difference that capitalizing operating leases makes. Capital employed with cash nearly doubles. Without cash, it *more* than doubles. None of this is unusual for a retailer.

Capitalizing operating leases can be easier in America than elsewhere. This is because the SEC mandates more detailed disclosures.[6] Companies in other countries can reveal less. Many are allowed to mash together the lease expenses scheduled for between two and five years into the future, for example.[7] Consider Gap competitor H&M, which is based in Sweden. It offers a blurrier glimpse of its future real estate commitments.[8] This compels the investor to guess more.

Not that our take on Gap's capital employed is rock solid. For one, it's good for one day only: January 30, 2016. That's the date of the balance sheet that the inputs come from. Actually, it's good for only a specific *time* on that day: the *close of business* on January 30, 2016.[9] What was capital employed that morning? The next week? We don't know.

Perishability is but one limitation of our appraisal of capital employed. Another is that it's based on old costs, which may or may not reflect replacement costs. Maybe that $1,000 bicycle goes for $1,100 now. Or $900. Imperfections abound, with capital employed and with other key numbers.

Such is investing. It's gussied up as a science, but it's nothing more than a lesser art. A *messy* lesser art, like fingerpainting. But it works because one has only to decide whether to buy, sell, or do nothing.

## CHAPTER 8

# Operating Income

| Do I understand it? | → | Is it good? |
|---|---|---|

Products
Customers
Industry
Form
Geography
Status

A second key number is *operating income*. It's right on the income statement. It sometimes appears as *operating earnings* or *operating profit*.

Chapter 6 sketched out the organization of the income statement. It starts with revenue, subtracts cost of goods sold, subtracts operating expenses, and ends with income. But as the LinkedIn case study showed, there are four different measures of income. Revisiting them makes clear why operating income is particularly useful.

Operating income is the topmost measure of income on the income statement. It's revenue, minus cost of goods sold, minus operating expenses.

To operating income one can then add—or subtract—*non-operating income*. Non-operating income is the gain or loss from activities that aren't part of what a company is *about*. They're business activities, but they're peripheral business activities. If the activities *made* money, something is *added* to operating income. If they *lost* money, something is *subtracted* from operating income. The result is the second measure of income: *earnings before interest and taxes*, or *EBIT*.

EBIT isn't necessarily a truer measure of income than is operating income. It's just *different*.

From EBIT one can then subtract *interest expense*. Interest isn't considered an *operating expense*, so it isn't captured in EBIT. Subtracting interest expense from EBIT yields the third measure of income: *earnings before tax*.

Subtracting tax expense from earnings before tax yields *net income*. It's the fourth measure of income. It's sometimes called *net earnings* or *net profit*. It's also called *the bottom line*, since there's nothing more left to subtract.

At first glance, net income seems like a perfectly good measure of the profitability of a business. It is, after all, the bottom line. So why focus on operating income? Because it makes comparisons easier. To see this, consider what operating income *ignores*.

For one, it ignores non-operating income, or those earnings that—by the company's own admission—aren't regular. Capturing the heart of a business's ongoing earnings is the goal, so activities that are tangential should be set aside.

It also ignores interest expense. Interest expense reflects how much debt is on the balance sheet, and how good a deal the company got from its lenders. It captures how a company was *financed*, not just how it operates.

Operating income also ignores taxes. Tax expenses reflect where a business is located. As noted earlier, tax rates vary among countries, and sometimes among states or provinces within those countries.

In other words, operating income measures the profitability of a business *without regard for the capital structure or tax regime in which it is trapped*.

How does this facilitate comparisons? In two ways.

First, it lets one compare the same enterprise at different points in time. Companies move. They recapitalize. A business in California might relocate to lower-tax Texas. A business that sits on a debt-free balance sheet might *lever up*. Tax rates and interest expenses can shift if management wants them to. But the basic economics of an industry are more fixed. Fiat isn't available as a means of changing the earnings capacity of a core operation. The measure of that earnings capacity is operating income.

Second, it lets one compare *different* businesses at the *same* point in time. It's the best measure of income for looking at companies that have different tax rates or debt situations, but are otherwise similar.

Consider food retailers. Loblaw, the largest supermarket chain in Canada, had an effective income tax rate in 2013 of 26.6 percent.[1] Kroger, the largest supermarket store chain in the United States, had an effective income tax rate in 2013 of 32.9 percent.[2] That's a big difference. It's born of a gap in tax policy between Canada and America.

A comparison between Loblaw and Kroger on the basis of *net income* would be colored by their locations. One's view of them *as grocers* would be clouded. But operating income makes it clear.

The same is true with debt. In 2013, Kroger paid $443,000,000 in interest on its long-term debt, which stood at $9,654,000,000 at year's end.[3] But Whole Foods Market, a supermarket chain based in Texas, paid *nothing* in interest expense. It ended 2013 with *no* financial debt.[4] A comparison of these two companies based on net income or earnings before tax would be steeped in this capital structure gap. Does one want to capture that in a first look at these businesses?

No. It would distort one's take on the core operations. Again, operating income emerges as a better primary indicator of income-generating power.

This is not to deny that a company has to pay interest, or that it has to pay taxes. Nor is it to suggest that interest and tax expense don't have an impact on shareholder returns. They do. But it's more instructive to *begin* by looking at what the heart of an enterprise produces (Figure 8.1).

When we start calculating metrics, we'll consider operating income and capital employed together. Adjustments shaping one must therefore shape the other. If operating leases were capitalized in the calculation of capital employed, some changes need to be made to the published operating income figure.

First, the lease expense needs to be added back. In a 10-K, this amount appears in a table following the financial statements. Search for the term *lease expense*, *rent expense*, or *rental expense*.

Second, a new depreciation expense needs to be subtracted. Recall that the capitalization of operating leases compels one to put new interest and depreciation expenses on the income statement. They're swapped *in* for the lease expense that's taken *out*. In fact, a common assumption is that the sum of the new interest and depreciation expenses *equals* the old lease expense. That is, *net income* doesn't change.

Interest expense isn't directly relevant to operating income, because it's lower down on the income statement. It's captured in *earnings before taxes* and *net income*, but not in operating income. But interest is the key to estimating depreciation, which *is* captured in operating income. So it has to be quantified.

When adjustments were made to capital employed, an interest rate was identified. It was an estimate of the rate at which the company could borrow money. It was used to calculate present value. Now, that same rate can be used to gauge interest expense.

Find the amount that was added to both sides of the balance sheet as the capitalized operating lease present value. Effectively, that's the size of the loan used to buy the equipment. Multiply that number by the interest rate. The result is the interest expense. Subtract this number from the old lease expense for the same year. The result is depreciation expense.

My focus on operating income comes from two things. First, I'm an American. My investment experience is in the United States. I routinely see funds take stakes in public companies, and then encourage those companies to better themselves. Sometimes this takes the form of a nudge, and sometimes it takes the form of a shove. But eventually many American companies get their tax situations and capital structures optimized.

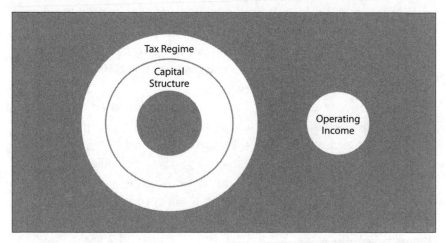

**FIGURE 8.1: Operating income measures the profitability of a business without regard for the capital structure or tax regime in which it is trapped.**

This happens in other countries as well, but to a lesser extent. Rules can limit the potency of institutional investor suggestions. Laws, customs, and cross-shareholdings can tie companies to particular locations, lenders, and capital structures.

Investors from such places won't share my preference for operating income, and justifiably so. To them tax and interest expenses are nearly as set as the basic economics of an industry. But operating income works for me because it's compatible with the broad range of tax and debt options available to the companies that I see.

The second thing that accounts for my focus on operating income is my long investment horizon. I hold stocks for decades. As far as I'm concerned, companies I own have years to get their taxes and capital structure in order. Someone with a target holding period of months wouldn't get this, and understandably so.

A few years ago I found in a relative's attic an old black-and-white stipple drawing. I like it. It's a moody Danish riverbank scene, with plump cows grazing under oaks. The only problem was that the drawing was set in a rotting frame of spindly wood with muddy, gold-colored trim. It underserved the art.

Fixing this was simple. I had the art reframed. It now sits inside a wide white mat surrounded by a black museum box frame. The piece hangs handsomely on the living room wall.

Some companies that I see are that stipple drawing in the old frame. The core operation—the drawing—is great. But the tax situation and the capital structure—the frame—is rotten. When will the frame get replaced? I have no idea. But others are likely to spot the virtues of the drawing and push for a reframing. My job is only to appreciate the art and to ready a space on the wall.

## Summary

1. Operating income is the best measure of the core earning capacity of a business.
2. Adjustments that shaped capital employed must also shape operating income.
3. If operating leases were capitalized, the calculation of operating income requires adding back an old lease expense and subtracting a new depreciation expense.

**CASE STUDY**

## The Gap, Inc., Part 2

Gap's income statement appears on page 35 of its 2015 10-K:

http://www.goodstockscheap.com/8.1.htm

Operating income is the fifth line down. For 2015, it's given as $1,524,000,000. But because capital employed was earlier adjusted to capitalize operating leases, two changes must be made.

First, lease expenses for 2015 need to be reversed. Lease expense isn't broken out on Gap's income statement. That's normal. And a search for the term "lease expense" turns up nothing. But "rent expense" gets 16 hits, one of which takes us back to note 11 on page 61. A table in the note reveals that net rent expense in 2015 was $1,313,000,000.[5]

Second, a new depreciation expense needs to be subtracted. Start by estimating interest expense. In the capital employed calculation, the present value of future lease expenses was determined to be $5,693,244,523. Take that to be the size of the loan.

The discount rate used in the present value calculation was 4 percent. This is presumed to equal the interest rate of the loan. So interest expense for 2015 is $227,729,781. That's just $5,693,244,523 times 4 percent.

Subtracting interest expense of $227,729,781 from the reversed lease expense of $1,313,000,000 yields $1,085,270,219. That's the depreciation expense.

Calculating operating income is now straightforward. Start with published operating income of $1,524,000,000, add back the old lease expense of $1,313,000,000, and subtract the new depreciation expense of $1,085,270,219. Gap's 2015 operating income is $1,751,729,781:

http://www.goodstockscheap.com/8.1.xlsx

## CHAPTER 9

# Free Cash Flow

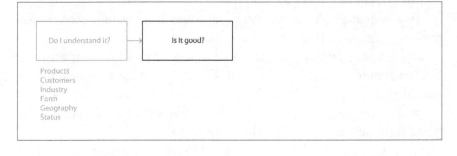

A third key number is *free cash flow*. It measures the amount of cash that a company *threw off* just by operating.

I calculate free cash flow by subtracting *capital expenditures* from *cash flow from operations*. Both of these numbers come from the cash flow statement.

Recall that a capital expenditure—also called *capex*—is the purchase of a noncurrent asset. There are two types: *maintenance capex* and *growth capex*. Maintenance capex is the purchase of equipment that will take over for equipment that is wearing out. It's *replacement*. It's an outlay that a company makes just to maintain its level of operations.

Growth capex is different. It's an outlay that a company makes to *expand* operations. It results in a bigger enterprise.

To calculate free cash flow well, only *maintenance* capex should be deducted from operating cash flow. After all, it's the cash-generating power of *present* operations that free cash flow aims to assess. It would be wrong to *underestimate* the performance of a business by subtracting *all* capex.

The problem is that cash flow statements don't divide capex into maintenance and growth.

A popular workaround is to accept depreciation—the accounting measure of how much capital equipment wore out—as a proxy for maintenance capex. This has merit, since deployed equipment depreciates. But I dislike this approach, for two reasons.

One is inflation. Depreciation is a portion of an *old* cost. It's a fraction of what *was* paid for a piece of capital equipment. That same piece of equipment might cost more now. Assuming that depreciation matches maintenance capex therefore introduces the risk of *underestimating* maintenance capex, and *overestimating* free cash flow. The company could look *better* than it is.

Two is quality. Pieces of equipment wearing out might be of *different quality* than their replacements.

Imagine a business that manufactures goods with four machines. Each machine cost $4,800 and is designed to last for four years. One machine was purchased at the start of the business's first year of operation, the second was purchased at the start of the second, the third at the third, and the fourth at the fourth.

On a *straight line* basis, each machine would depreciate $1,200 per year. That's just $4,800 divided by four. In year four—with all four machines in service—total depreciation would equal $4,800.

Say that at the end of year four, the first machine wears out right on schedule. Assume that the business replaces it with a *cheaper* machine. The cheaper machine makes just as many goods annually as the old one did, but it has half the life span. It costs only $2,000 and will last for just two years. On a straight line basis, it depreciates only $1,000 per year.

What would total depreciation be in year *five*? There would be three old machines in use, and one new. Total depreciation for the three old machines would be $1,200 times three, or $3,600. Depreciation for the one new machine would be $1,000. So total year five deprecation would be $4,600.

But what was maintenance capex in year five? It was the cost of the one new machine: $2,000. It was *less than half* of depreciation.

Had the business bought one of the *old* models as a replacement, maintenance capex and depreciation would be closer. But the business bought a *different kind* of machine. This made depreciation

higher than maintenance capex, which could lead to an un
tion of free cash flow. The company could look worse than

A workaround better than relying on depreciation is to search for
some breakout of maintenance capex in a 10-K. Another is to listen
for one during webcast *earnings calls*. These are recordings of quarterly telephone meetings between management and equity analysts.
One can listen to them for free on company websites.

The prepared remarks that dominate the first part of an earnings
call are unhelpful. It's storytime. But the question and answer session
that follows can unearth nuggets. Sometimes a maintenance capex
figure pops up.

When both of these approaches fail me, I pretend that all capex is
maintenance capex, knowing that I'm painting an overly dark picture
of the enterprise. I prefer to assume the worst with the prospect of
delight than to assume the best with the likelihood of disappointment.

Any adjustments that shaped *capital employed* and *operating
income* should also shape free cash flow. So if one capitalized operating leases, one must make two adjustments.

First, lease payments should be added back to *cash flow from
operations*. Assume that lease payments equal the lease expense
that was added back to published operating income. That is, lease
payments can be considered to have been made right when they
were due.

Note that the terms *expense* and *payment* are related, but they're
not synonymous. Expense is associated with *accrual* accounting and
the *income statement*. Payment is associated with *cash* accounting
and the *cash flow statement*.

Second, interest payments on the pretend loan should be subtracted
from cash flow from operations. The amount to subtract equals the
interest expense that was estimated in the calculation of operating
income. As with lease payments, interest payments can be assumed
to have been made when due.

This teases out an accounting point. Some companies that report
under IFRS put interest payments not in *cash flow from operations*,
but rather in *cash flow from financing*. If one capitalized the operating leases of such a company, one should not only subtract the new
interest payments, but also move existing interest payments from the
financing section to the operations section.

This formula for free cash flow—*cash flow from operations* minus *capex*, adjusted for the capitalization of operating leases—yields a specific measure of free cash flow. It's called *levered free cash flow*. Levered means indebted. It indicates the inclusion of interest payments.

*Unlevered free cash flow* is different. It excludes interest payments. To calculate it, first add interest payments back to levered free cash flow. Include both interest payments created when operating leases were capitalized, and any interest payments that existed beforehand.

Second, increase tax payments. Interest is a tax-deductible expense. So erasing interest expense boosts *earnings before taxes*, compelling the company to pay more income tax.

This is relevant because both US GAAP and IFRS place tax payments in cash flow from *operations*. An exception to this is under IFRS with tax payments on specific investing and financing activities.

It's simple to calculate how much tax payments should go up. Start by finding the company's income tax rate. Search the 10-K for the term *effective tax rate* or, failing that, just *tax rate*. Then, subtract that percentage from 100 percent. If the tax rate was 30 percent, then the number is 70 percent. Finally, multiply that number by the interest payments that were added back. That's how much tax payments should increase.

Which is more useful, *levered free cash flow* or *unlevered free cash flow*?

I prefer levered free cash flow because it gives me such a different look at a company than does *operating income*. Operating income is an *accrual* accounting figure that *ignores* taxes and interest, while levered free cash flow is a *cash* accounting figure that *captures* taxes and interest. Together, these two perspectives help me to see everything important related to how much money came out of a business.

Another question. What's higher: operating income, or *unlevered* free cash flow?

Both overlook interest. But unlevered free cash flow captures tax payments, while operating income ignores tax expenses. So operating income would usually be higher. But if tax payments were added back to unlevered free cash flow, now which would be higher?

Still operating income. Understanding why is useful.

Most businesses have a *normal cash cycle*. They *pay* before they *get paid*. They disburse cash to lease space, pay employees, and buy raw materials. Then they deliver products to customers who pay *afterward*. As such, revenue is recognized on the income statement *before* the associated inflows from operations happen on the cash flow statement. This is particularly true with growing businesses. More and more cash is outlayed as companies build.

With shrinking businesses, the reverse can be true. Operating income can be *lower*. Cash from previously large order bases pours in as input purchases slow. But most companies worthy of an investor's attention do more growing than shrinking.

Occasionally a company's business model creates a *negative cash cycle*. This happy situation has a company getting paid by customers *before* it pays vendors. An example is a magazine publisher that requires prepayment for subscriptions. Unlevered free cash flow can exceed operating income even though the business is growing.

But besides those that are paid in advance and those that are in decline, businesses normally see revenue exceed cash inflows from operations. This will become important when we start measuring past performance. We'll hold metrics based on *free cash flow* to a lower standard than those based on *operating income*.

Free cash flow—levered or unlevered—and operating income are equally useful numbers. One isn't superior to the other. They're just *different*. Considering both brings the knowable closer to the known.

## Summary

1. Free cash flow equals cash flow from operations minus maintenance capex.
2. If maintenance capex isn't distinguishable from growth capex, subtracting all capex is a conservative—though imperfect—approach.
3. If operating leases were capitalized, the calculation of free cash flow requires adding back an old lease payment and subtracting a new interest payment.
4. Levered free cash flow captures interest payments, while unlevered free cash flow does not.
5. Most businesses have a normal cash cycle.

## The Gap, Inc., Part 3

Gap's cash flow statement appears on page 38 of its 2015 10-K:

http://www.goodstockscheap.com/9.1.htm

*Cash flow from operations*—which Gap calls *net cash provided by operating activities*—was $1,594,000,000 in 2015.

Capital expenditures—*purchases of property and equipment*—was $726,000,000 in 2015. As usual, the cash flow statement makes no distinction between maintenance and growth capex. And a search for the terms *maintenance* and *growth* in the document turns up nothing relevant.

On February 25, 2016, Gap held an earnings call with equity analysts to discuss the company's 2015 results. Unfortunately, no estimate of maintenance capex was mentioned.[1]

Therefore, a conservative approach is to subtract all capex. Is there a way to estimate how much this will understate free cash flow?

Yes. Depreciation and maintenance capex are different, as noted earlier. But comparing depreciation to total capex gives some sense of how gross the divergence could be.

Search the document for the term *depreciation*. A hit at the bottom of page 47 reveals that depreciation expense for property and equipment was $588,000,000 in 2015. That's 81 percent of the $726,000,000 capex figure. So it's not *hugely* different. Free cash flow may wind up understated, but not obscenely.

We earlier capitalized Gap's operating leases. Hence, lease payments need to be added back. The lease expense that was added back to published operating income was $1,313,000,000. That's the number to use.

Also, interest payments must be subtracted. The amount to use equals the interest expense that was estimated in the calculation of operating income. That was $227,729,781.

Gap's 2015 levered free cash flow can now be approximated. It's *cash flow from operations* of $1,594,000,000, minus *capex* of

$726,000,000, plus the old lease payments of $1,313,000,000, minus the new interest expense of $227,729,781. That equals $1,953,270,219.

Calculating *unlevered* free cash flow is also straightforward. First add back the just-added interest expense of $227,729,781 to levered free cash flow. Then add back any interest payments that existed beforehand. They can be assumed to equal interest expenses. Gap's income statement on page 35 reveals that 2015 interest expense was $59,000,000. So total interest to add back is $286,729,781. That's just $227,729,781 plus $59,000,000.

Next, increase tax payments to capture the loss of the tax deduction from interest. A search for the term *effective tax rate* leads to page 23, which shows it was 37.5 percent in 2015. Subtracting that percentage from 100 percent yields 62.5 percent. Total interest added back of $286,729,781 times 62.5 percent equals $179,206,113. That's the tax to subtract.

Therefore, Gap's 2015 unlevered free cash flow equals $2,060,793,887. That's *levered free cash flow* of $1,953,270,219, plus total interest payments of $286,729,781, minus additional tax payments of $179,206,113:[2]

http://www.goodstockscheap.com/9.1.xlsx

# CHAPTER 10

# Book Values and Shares

A fourth key number is *book value*. Earlier, we used this term to describe the purchase price less depreciation of a noncurrent asset. When applied to a whole company, book value means *equity*. It's right on the balance sheet. It's the company's worth from a formal accounting perspective.

Equity is assets minus liabilities. But sometimes, the balance sheet has an equity line that's *smaller* than assets minus liabilities. This came up with LinkedIn. Its China subsidiary had a minority partner. The partner owned a piece of the business that a LinkedIn public shareholder wouldn't. This piece appeared in the equity section of the balance sheet as *redeemable noncontrolling interest*.

Noncontrolling interests—redeemable or not—are normal. They're the difference between *shareholders' equity* and the larger *total shareholders' equity*. It's the former, smaller number that the astute investor takes to equal book value. It better represents the size of the pie that one could buy a slice of.

Two things make equity go up. One is *retained earnings*, which as noted earlier is *net income* not paid out as dividends. Another is the issuance of new stock for cash.

Correspondingly, two things make equity go down. One is the payment of dividends. Another is share *repurchases*. Also called *buybacks*, they're the opposite of new stock issuances. They're the company buying back its own stock for cash. On the balance sheet, they're accounted for by a decrease in cash *with no corresponding increase in another asset*. Hence, to keep the balance sheet in balance, they make shareholders' equity go down.

This means that any metric based on book value is influenced by repurchases. This isn't automatically good or bad. It's just something to be aware of, as we'll see.

A fifth key number is *tangible book value*. It's book value minus *intangible assets*. Intangible assets are any assets that aren't physical. They include goodwill, trademarks, and patents. They're broken out in the asset sections of balance sheets at varying levels of detail.

Tangible book value is the company's worth from an *even stricter* formal accounting perspective. Not only does it disregard the value of ongoing operations, it disregards the value of anything that can't be touched.

It's old-fashioned. Tangible book value recalls an era when financial statements were less reliable and less frequently published, a time when physical assets were thought to embody an enterprise's bankability.

I find tangible book value useful for flagging companies that overpay for acquisitions. If book value is much higher than tangible book value, it's often because goodwill is enormous. This directs my attention to the company's acquisition history. If it recently bought another public company, I analyze the acquired company *right before the acquisition*. I look at its old 10-K. Would I have paid that price? If not, I stop my analysis. I don't care what the purported synergies were. Overpriced acquisitions are the beginning of a story that ends poorly. I'm not in it.

A sixth and final key number is *shares*. Many useful metrics are expressed on a *per-share basis*. They capture the dilutive effect of an increase in the number of shares, or the concentrating effect of a decrease in the number of shares.

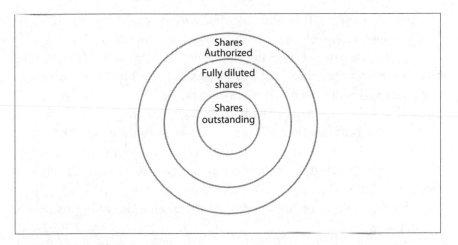

**FIGURE 10.1: Share counts**

The utility of this is clear. It's one thing to say that operating income increased from $1,000,000 last year to $2,000,000 this year. But if the number of shares doubled over the same period, it's important to note that operating income *per share* remained flat.

How does one count the number of shares? An annual report often puts forth several different measures (Figure 10.1). One is *shares outstanding*. Sometimes it's called *basic shares*. It's the number of shares that people, investment funds, and other entities hold.

Another measure is *fully diluted shares*. It's a bigger number. It's shares outstanding plus the number of shares that *could* become outstanding if other securities issued by the company were *exercised* or *converted*. For example, the exercise of a *warrant* would lead to an increase in the number of shares outstanding, as would the conversion of a *convertible bond*. An employee exercising stock options would have the same effect.

A third measure is *shares authorized*. It's bigger still. It's the number of shares that a company is *allowed* to issue according to its charter or bylaws. It equals the number of fully diluted shares plus shares that *could* come into existence because of the issuance of new stock, warrants, options, or convertible bonds.

Which to choose? Many pick shares outstanding. But when considering the purchase of a stock, I prefer fully diluted shares. This is because in a successful company, *anything that can become a share will become a share.*

Employees will exercise their options. Bondholders who can will convert. Warrantholders will exercise. They'll all do these things so they can sell stock at newly high prices. This is why fully diluted shares becomes the most meaningful denominator.

Using authorized shares might seem even more forthright, since it's an even larger number. But that would be overkill. It's a major decision for a company to issue new stock that it doesn't have to because of a conversion or an exercise. It doesn't naturally happen. So it shouldn't be assumed to be the eventual number of shares outstanding.

The number of fully diluted shares is easy to find in a 10-K or annual report. It appears either toward the bottom of the income statement or in the notes to the financial statements. Search the document for the word *diluted*. Only chemical companies use that term to mean anything else.

The fully diluted shares measure isn't perfect. For instance, it doesn't take into account the cash the company could receive in the event of conversions. Exercising stock options, for example, often entails the payment of a *strike price* by the option holder. This would lead to a *cash inflow from financing* for the company, and an uptick in the company's cash balance. But unless one knows the strike price, capturing this effect is difficult.

Here's another one. During the course of a year, the number of fully diluted shares fluctuates. *Secondary offerings* happen, options get issued, and the number of shares generally bops around. This is particularly true in the United States.

To capture this variability, annual reports often report the *weighted average* number of fully diluted shares. This is the number of fully diluted shares weighted by *time*. Sometimes it's lower than the number of fully diluted shares at the *end* of the reporting period. Other times, it's higher. But again, this is an imperfection that one can live with.

## Summary

1. Book value equals equity excluding noncontrolling interests.
2. Tangible book value equals book value less all nonphysical assets.
3. Fully diluted shares is the most meaningful of the three share counts.

---

**CASE STUDY**

### The Gap, Inc., Part 4

Gap's 2015 balance sheet is on page 34 of its 10-K:

http://www.goodstockscheap.com/10.1.htm

The second line from the bottom reads *total stockholders' equity*. It's $2,545,000,000. There's no other equity line on the balance sheet, and no mention of a noncontrolling interest. So that's book value. Easy.

Tangible book value is straightforward to calculate. The assets section of Gap's balance sheet makes no mention of goodwill, trademarks, patents, or any other common intangible asset. So they're probably buried in one of the larger asset lines, like *other long-term assets*.

Search for the word *intangible*. One hit is *note 3* on page 49. It says that on January 30, 2016—the last day of Gap's 2015 fiscal year, and the same day as the balance sheet—*goodwill* was $180,000,000, *trade names* was $92,000,000, *other indefinite-lived intangible assets* was $4,000,000, and *intangible assets subject to amortization, net* was $1,000,000. The sum of these four numbers is $277,000,000.

We know what goodwill is. But what are those other things?

Earlier we defined goodwill as *acquisition price in excess of equity*. That's basically true. But sometimes when one company buys another, part of the excess acquisition price gets allocated to intangible asset categories *other* than goodwill.

*Trade names*, for example. Trade names are *brands*. In Gap's case the brands are Athleta and Intermix, the names of two companies Gap had recently acquired.

What about *other indefinite-lived intangible assets*? Goodwill and trade names are the best examples of indefinite-lived intangible assets. So it's unclear what this is. Not that it matters; $4,000,000 is a relatively small amount. But digging into the phrase is instructive.

*Indefinite-lived* means *not amortized*. Recall that amortization is like depreciation, but for an intangible asset. It's accounting's way of capturing the loss in worth over time of something that can't be touched. So like goodwill and trade names, whatever is in this line doesn't automatically tick down in worth each year.

This contrasts with *intangible assets subject to amortization, net*, which does. Page 49 says that this line includes "customer relationships and non-compete agreements."

*Customer relationships* are an acquired asset because they produce economic benefits—sales—over some period of time.

*Non-compete agreements* are promises made by people from Athleta and Intermix to hold off a while before starting—or joining—a rival of their new parent company. The agreements last for a limited period of time, so amortization is the right tool for periodically reducing their worth.

Gap's tangible book value at the end of fiscal 2015 was $2,268,000,000. That's just book value of $2,545,000,000 minus total intangible assets of $277,000,000.

The number of fully diluted shares is easy to find. A search for *diluted* leads to *item 6* on page 16. It gives the *weighted-average number of shares—diluted* as 413,000,000. This number also appears toward the bottom of the income statement on page 35, and then later in the notes, as it should.[1]

## CHAPTER 11

# Past Performance

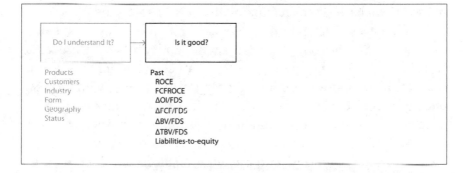

| Do I understand It? | Is it good? |
|---|---|
| Products | Past |
| Customers | ROCE |
| Industry | FCFROCE |
| Form | ΔOI/FDS |
| Geography | ΔFCF/FDS |
| Status | ΔBV/FDS |
| | ΔTBV/FDS |
| | Liabilities-to-equity |

Extracting key numbers from financial statements lets one calculate *performance metrics*. There are seven. They make clear whether or not a business has been historically good.

The first performance metric is *return on capital employed*, or *ROCE*. ROCE is a ratio. It's expressed as a percentage. The numerator is *operating income*. The denominator is *capital employed*.

The purpose of ROCE is to show how much money a business *made* relative to the amount of capital it *needed*.

The numerator, operating income, describes a *period* of time. This is because it comes from the income statement, which is like a movie.

But the denominator, capital employed, describes a *point* in time. It's calculated from the balance sheet, which is like a snapshot. This leads to a question. What point during a year best reflects the capital employed that produced annual operating income?

This matters. Capital employed can change a lot over 12 months. Total assets, cash balances, and non-interest-bearing current liabilities all fluctuate.

There are three choices. One is the *beginning* of the year. This means calculating capital employed from the *prior* year's ending balance sheet. Another is the *end* of the year, which means using the current year's ending balance sheet. A third is to use an average, by taking the arithmetic mean of the beginning and the end.

One could also toy with the balance sheet figures from quarterly reports. But quarterly figures are unaudited, and as such less solid.

Absent some special insight, one method is to calculate two versions of capital employed: one at the beginning of the year, and one at the end of the year. This yields a range of possible values. This echoes our approach to cash, where we measured capital employed both with *no* cash subtracted and with *all* cash subtracted.

I like ranges. They remind me of how rough even my best calculations are. So for a single period I wind up with *four* measures of ROCE. Each is defined by my treatment of capital employed: beginning of the period with cash, beginning of the period without cash, end of the period with cash, and end of the period without cash. We'll cover which is most useful, and how to benchmark it, shortly.

A second performance metric is *free cash flow return on capital employed*. I abbreviate it to the unpronounceable *FCFROCE*. It's levered free cash flow divided by capital employed.

Like ROCE, FCFROCE requires picking a date on which to measure capital employed. Using a range again makes sense. As with ROCE, one comes up with a total of four measures of FCFROCE, each defined by the treatment of cash and time in the denominator.

In a growing business, FCFROCE will often be lower than ROCE. This is because levered free cash flow tends to lag operating income. It captures interest, tax, and the normal cash cycle. Operating income doesn't.

A third performance metric is *growth in operating income per fully diluted share*. I shorten it to ΔOI/FDS. In using Δ—the Greek letter *delta*—I'm not trying to be fancy. I use it for the practical reason that it means *change*. It nicely captures the possibility that growth could be either positive or negative.

Calculating ΔOI/FDS is easy. Divide operating income by fully diluted shares for the first year. Then do the same for the second. Next, subtract the first from the second, and divide the result by the first. A percentage results.

If operating income per fully diluted share was $3 in 2015 and $4 in 2016, ΔOI/FDS in 2016 was 33 percent. That's just ($4 − $3)/$3.

The fourth performance metric is *growth in free cash flow per fully diluted share*. It's abbreviated ΔFCF/FDS. It's computed by dividing levered free cash flow by the number of fully diluted shares for the first year, then doing the same for the second. Then, subtract the first from the second, and divide the result by the first.

The fifth performance metric is *growth in book value per fully diluted share*. Shortened, it's ΔBV/FDS. The calculation is by now familiar. Divide book value by the number of fully diluted shares for the first year, then do the same for second. Then, subtract the first from the second, and divide the result by the first.

The metric ΔBV/FDS shows the increase in worth over time from a strict accounting standpoint. But it has limited utility by itself. This is for two reasons. One, it fails to capture dividends. Dividends come directly out of book value. So meaningfully using ΔBV/FDS requires knowing about any dividends paid.

While book value growth and dividends are both related to an investor's return, they're different. It would be wrong to regard a dollar of one as *equivalent* to a dollar of the other. This is in part because dividends are usually taxed, while growth in book value usually isn't. So it would be overly simplistic to lump the two together in a single operating metric.

Another reason that ΔBV/FDS has limited utility by itself is because it's influenced by share repurchases. Buybacks can make ΔBV/FDS negative even if a company has positive ΔOI/FDS and pays no dividends. The metric is nonetheless worth calculating, as will be shown later.

The sixth performance metric is *growth in tangible book value per fully diluted share*, or ΔTBV/FDS. Predictably, it's calculated by dividing tangible book value by the number of fully diluted shares for the first year, then doing the same for the second year. Then subtract the first from the second, and divide the result by the first. This metric has merit, but it too doesn't capture dividends and is influenced by buybacks. So again, it's of limited use by itself.

The seventh performance metric is the *liabilities-to-equity ratio*. It sizes the prominence of obligations on a company's balance sheet. It's computed by dividing total liabilities by book value.

Most good investors take some measure of a company's indebtedness. Many use the *interest coverage ratio*. It equals EBIT divided by interest expense. It measures a company's ability to *service*—or *pay interest on*—its debt.

Others use the *debt-to-equity ratio*. The numerator is the company's *financial* obligations. These are bonds, bank loans, and other *interest-bearing* liabilities.

I maniacally expand the numerator to include *all* liabilities: bonds, bank loans, accounts payable, accrued expenses, unearned revenue—anything owed, interest-bearing or not. Why? Because companies can crumble under the weight of too many obligations of any kind. I want that captured in my metric. Again, my goal is to see if a company looks good in the dimmest possible light. I'm a worst-case scenario *addict*.

While I prefer the liabilities-to-equity ratio, the alternatives can work well too. What's important is to consider a company's indebtedness in some way. Here's why.

Liabilities amplify results. If things go well for a highly leveraged company, they go *really well*. The economic benefits of success gush in the direction of the shareholders, because the debtholders and vendors have limited upside. Lenders get their interest and principal back, and vendors get paid. But that's it. Their upsides have ceilings.

Shareholders have no ceiling. The sky is their limit. This ceilinglessness often takes the form of an increasing stock price.

But if things go poorly for a highly leveraged company, they go *quite poorly*. Operating income falters and cash flow slows to a trickle, but the liability burden lets up not one iota. Lenders demand their interest and principal. Vendors want their invoices paid. Insolvency can result. It's this technical possibility of disaster that tilts value investors toward businesses with manageable obligations.

A high liabilities-to-equity ratio may be palatable in two cases. One is when a very creditworthy company has a high-return use for cash borrowed in a time of low interest rates. Another is when equity has been reduced through dividends or—under certain circumstances, defined later—buybacks.

Occasionally these two conditions combine. A strong company borrows money at a low interest rate to buy back its stock at prices well below value. Debt soars and book value condenses, creating a grotesquely high liabilities-to-equity ratio. But the situation may nonetheless be attractive to the astute investor.

Sometimes a company has an irregular year. A spike in demand could juice earnings. A recession could plunge cash flow. It would be misleading to judge a company based on one such year. At the same time, it would be foolish to pretend that it didn't happen. What one really wants is to make judgments based on *normalized* results.

One way to normalize results is to look at several years together. Consider ROCE. If a business hasn't fundamentally changed over the last five years, one could calculate *average* ROCE by adding up the operating income of all five years, and dividing that number by the sum of each year's capital employed.

With four varieties of capital employed for each year—beginning of the period with cash, beginning of the period without cash, end of the period with cash, and end of the period without cash—one would wind up with four measures of average ROCE.

Average FCFROCE can be calculated in the same way.

Growth metrics can also be averaged over several years. But the arithmetic mean doesn't work with growth data, because it fails to capture compounding. One should instead use the *geometric mean*. We used this in Chapter 4 to assess investment performance.

I like normalizing by taking multiyear averages. But some prefer doing so by tweaking individual years. They remove atypical events. By this method a one-time litigation settlement expense, for example, would get added back. I dislike this approach, for three reasons.

First, only future periods can determine what's truly irregular. Was that litigation expense really a one-off? If it happens again, no.

Second, to the extent that there are real irregularities, management-level knowledge is required to identify them. Annual reports, press releases, and news items are detailed enough to fool outside investors into thinking that they can spot them too. But they can't.

Third, *every* year has irregularities of one sort or another. Once one starts tweaking, there's no end to the justifiable tweakings.

For these three reasons I prefer to regard historic operating performance as just that: *historic*. I don't try to clean it up and pretend that its sanitized version will repeat.

With the liabilities-to-equity ratio, normalization doesn't make sense. What matters is the most recent version of that figure. If the ratio was lower last year than it is now, that fact makes the weight of present obligations no less burdensome.

When we calculate the seven performance metrics, we wind up with actual numbers. Consider ROCE. It may be 9 percent, or 19 percent. What's good, and what isn't? The answer can be found in the stock market.

Since the year of my birth—1967—the stock market has returned 10.2 percent per year on average. That's the geometric mean of the S&P 500 total return from 1967 to 2015. One could get that performance with a simple low-cost index fund, like Vanguard's VFINX.

Chapter 2 noted that good investors often do fundamental analysis with the mindset that they're buying the *entire* company. Adopt that perspective now. Picture buying *all* of the shares and delisting the company from the stock exchange. No more stock quotes. As the years rolled on, what kind of return could one expect?

One would get all of the company's net income. Over time, that figure would accurately reflect—via depreciation—the cost of replacing equipment wearing out, or *maintenance capex*. As the years rolled on, this relationship between net income and capital employed would come to govern one's return. If that figure isn't at least 10.2 percent annually, the company isn't worth buying. After all, VFINX can do that.

Of course ROCE doesn't use *net income* as its numerator, but rather the larger *operating income*. This excludes tax and interest expense. So 10.2 percent is too low a benchmark for ROCE. Instead I use 15 percent. That's my rough estimate of the average annual S&P 500 total return if none of its component companies had to pay interest or taxes.

It may be unintuitive why ROCE can be meaningfully benchmarked against a stock market average. After all, ROCE has nothing to do with the price paid for shares, while stock market returns have a lot to do with that. The explanation can be found by taking the long-term view.

Inflation is powerful. It causes a company's operating numbers—income, replacement equipment costs—to go up. But the price paid for the company doesn't go up. It's *history*. Inflation causes that price to look smaller and smaller as it fades into the past.

If an investor pays $7,000,000 for a company that generated operating income of $1,000,000 last year, the price initially feels like a meaningful multiple of earnings. But after—say—three decades, when operating income is—say—$2,500,000, the original purchase price seems almost *cute*.

Incidentally, $1,000,000 to $2,500,000 over three decades implies an annual growth rate of around 3 percent. That's just inflation. If there was real growth in the business, that original $7,000,000 purchase price could seem *very cute*.

What about FCFROCE? It can be benchmarked against a stock market return for the same reasons. But 10.2 percent is too high, because of the normal cash cycle. I use 8 percent.

Growth metrics also need benchmarks: ΔOI/FDS could come in at 1 percent, or 11 percent; ΔFCF/FDS could be 4 percent, or 14 percent. What's good?

As an absolute baseline, consider inflation. As noted, U.S. inflation has averaged around 3 percent in recent decades. So if we're looking at a growth rate under 3 percent, we're probably looking at a business that's *shrinking*. That's because financial statement figures are *nominal*. They're not adjusted for inflation. So in *real* terms, the business isn't growing at all.

This is not to say that 4 percent indicates an exciting growth story. Higher benchmarks are appropriate. But opinions vary as to how much higher.

Benchmarking the liability-to-equity ratio is much harder. This is both because of the distorting effect of buybacks, and because interest costs can vary so much among companies. As a general rule I like it to be no higher than 2. But if all of the other performance metrics are great and the company is using cheap borrowed money to buy back its underpriced stock, I can be comfortable with a ratio as high as 7.

With spreadsheets, calculating all seven performance metrics is straightforward. There are really only about a dozen figures that need to be pulled from the financial statements for each year. From the income statement, there's operating income, and possibly interest expense. From the cash flow statement, there's cash flow from operations, and capital expenditures. From the balance sheet, there's cash, goodwill, intangible assets, total assets, accounts payable, deferred income, accrued expenses, total liabilities, and shareholders' equity. The only additional figures needed are the number of fully diluted shares and maybe the effective tax rate.

Sometimes it's easier. Several of the figures—deferred income and accrued liabilities, for example—may already be combined onto a single line. Other times it's harder, like when operating leases need to be capitalized. But on balance the process is manageable, and worth the breadth of historical detail that the numbers can be made to reveal.

Sometimes a performance metric is negative. Average FCFROCE or ΔOI/FDS may be minus. Other times, a performance metric may be simply underwhelming. ROCE may be 7 percent, or ΔFCF/FDS may be 1 percent with no other compensating growth metric. Avoid making excuses for unremarkable companies. The value investing model is designed to flag them. If a business looks bad, consider it no further. There are others more worthy of attention.

Remember that performance metrics are historical. They measure how things *went*. If a growth rate comes in at 10 percent, that means that something *grew* at 10 percent, not necessarily that it's *growing* at 10 percent. The future may not replicate the past. We'll next introduce a wholly different set of tools to see how things are likely to turn out going forward.

## Summary

A business's historic performance can be measured with seven metrics:

1. Return on capital employed (ROCE)
2. Free cash flow return on capital employed (FCFROCE)
3. Growth in operating income per fully diluted share (ΔOI/FDS)
4. Growth in free cash flow per fully diluted share (ΔFCF/FDS)
5. Growth in book value per fully diluted share (ΔBV/FDS)
6. Growth in tangible book value per fully diluted share (ΔTBV/FDS)
7. Liabilities-to-equity ratio

| CASE STUDY |
| :---: |

## The Gap, Inc., Part 5

Calculating the seven historic operating metrics for Gap is straight-forward. We already have key numbers for 2015 from Chapters 7 through 10. Add to that key numbers for earlier years so that results can be normalized by taking averages. I went back to 2011:

> http://www.goodstockscheap.com/11.1.xlsx

First is ROCE. The numerator is operating income. In Chapter 8 we determined that this number—adjusted for capitalized operating leases—was $1,751,729,781 in 2015. When I add to this operating income from the four prior years—also all adjusted for capitalized operating leases—I get $10,345,414,998. That's the numerator for a *five*-year period.

The most recent *four*-year numerator should also be calculated, for reasons that will be clear in a moment. It's $8,643,310,597.

The denominator is capital employed. There are four versions, all with operating leases capitalized. Summing together 2011 through 2015, end of period *with* cash is $55,993,144,241, and end of period *without* cash is $48,253,144,241. Note that these are both for *five*-year periods. Their numerator must therefore be five years' worth of operating income.

Since a beginning of the year figure is based on the *prior* year's balance sheet, and I didn't pull data from 2010, I only have *four* years to sum for *beginning* capital employed. So beginning of the period with cash is $44,191,899,718, and beginning of the period without cash is $37,821,899,718. The appropriate numerator for these is *four* year's worth of operating income.

My four measures of ROCE come out to 18 percent, 21 percent, 20 percent, and 23 percent. That is, the *worst* average ROCE figure is 18 percent. That's still well above my benchmark of 15 percent. So I'm still interested in Gap.

Second is FCFROCE. The numerator is leveraged free cash flow. Adjusted for capitalized operating leases, the five-year sum is $10,521,585,002, and the four-year sum is $8,783,689,403. So the four averages come out to 19 percent, 21 percent, 20 percent, and 23 percent. The lowest, 19 percent, is still wildly above my benchmark of 8 percent. I remain interested.

Third is ΔOI/FDS. Since I pulled data for five years, I'm able to calculate four year-over-year growth rates: 2011 to 2012, 2012 to 2013, 2013 to 2014, and 2014 to 2015. When I take the geometric mean of these four, I get 7 percent. That's well over the rate of inflation, so the business seems not to be shrinking. But it did in 2015, when ΔOI/FDS was negative 19 percent.

A picture starts to emerge of a highly profitable business that, for reasons not yet determined, stopped growing.

Fourth is ΔFCF/FDS. The four-year average comes out to 10 percent. That's better, and well above the rate of inflation. But 2015 saw ΔFCF/FDS of negative 17 percent. The image of a profitable yet slipping business continues to develop.

Fifth is ΔBV/FDS. The four-year average is 4 percent, barely above the rate of inflation. Are buybacks tamping down the numerator? Yes. Page 15 of the 2015 10-K details a big repurchasing program. What about dividends? Also yes. Page 13 outs these book value thieves. Did ΔBV/FDS drop in 2015 like the other growth metrics? Yes again. It was negative 9 percent.

Given all that's going on, it may be hard to draw a finite conclusion from ΔBV/FDS. But recognizing a metric as unhelpful in a particular case can be as valuable as its leading to a conclusion.

Sixth is ΔTBV/FDS. The four-year average is 3 percent, and 2015 by itself is negative 11 percent. That's low. But again, there's a lot distorting equity.

Seventh is the *liabilities-to-equity ratio*. The 2015 balance sheet shows *total current liabilities* as $2,535,000,000, and *total long-term liabilities* as $2,393,000,000. Adding these together yields total liabilities of $4,928,000,000. Subtracting *total stockholders' equity* of $2,545,000,000 from *total assets* of $7,473,000,000 gives the same result, as it should.

Total liabilities divided by total stockholders' equity equals 194 percent. In other words, Gap has almost twice as many liabilities as it has equity. Is that high? Not really, especially in the low interest rate environment that recently let Gap borrow $400,000,000 at one percent, as we saw in Chapter 7. Plus, Gap's buyback program has shrunk its equity base, increasing the ratio.[1]

But it could actually be higher. One could decide to fluff up the numerator to include the present value of capitalized operating leases. After all, that's the estimate of an obligation. That would take liabilities way up to $10,621,244,523, and the liabilities-to-equity ratio up to 417 percent.

Overall, Gap's historic operating metrics paint a clear picture. The business has above-average profitability, and its liabilities may be manageable. But it stopped growing. Its attractiveness as an investment, then, hinges in part on whether or not growth is likely to return. This is the sort of question that the value investing model later addresses. The numbers not only tell a story, they say where to look next.

Some readers may take issue with my Gap calculations. They may find my discount rates too low, for example, or too high.

This is to be expected. There are hundreds of tiny judgments that go into the quantitative analysis of a single company. It's statistically improbable that someone would find *nothing* to question. What's important is that I lay plain what my choices were so that one's own decisions can be better made.

## CHAPTER 12

# Future Performance

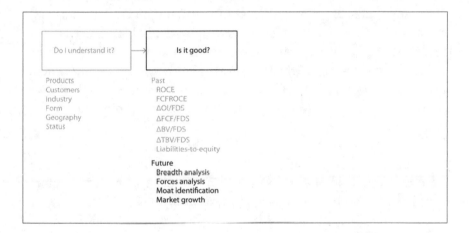

If a business has been historically good, the next step is to see if it's likely to remain so. This is harder, because accounting results for *future* periods don't exist, obviously. So instead one turns to *strategic analysis*. Specifically, four qualitative tools help to assess a firm's prospects.

The first is what I call *breadth analysis*. It asks two questions. One, is the company's customer base broad, and unlikely to consolidate? And two, is the company's supplier base broad, and unlikely to consolidate? The business isn't good unless the answer to both is *yes*.

I define a broad customer base as one where no single customer accounts for over a tenth of revenue. Similarly, I define a broad supplier base as one where no single supplier accounts for over a tenth of cost of goods sold or operating expenses.

It's easy to see why sustainably broad customer and supplier bases are important. If a company had only two customers, each accounting for half of sales, then the loss of one would devastate revenue. It wouldn't matter what the *cause* of the loss was, or if the company somehow *deserved it*. That it *happened* would be enough.

But if a company had a thousand customers, each accounting for a thousandth of revenue, the loss of a single customer would barely register. A good enterprise would try to understand why the customer left, of course. But it could comfortably absorb the short-term financial effect.

Same with supply. If only one vendor can provide a key raw material, any interruption in deliveries is a problem.

There's one exception. A good company may consciously concentrate purchases on a limited number of suppliers. This can yield bulk discounts and service concessions not available otherwise. But it can also cause one supplier to emerge as disproportionately important. Nonetheless, the company can still enjoy the economic benefits of a broad supplier base if several *potential* vendors stand ready to serve it. Alternative sources keep the favored supplier on its best behavior.

Analyzing customer breadth is straightforward. Annual reports often contain a clear statement like "no single customer accounted for over 10 percent of our revenue." The absence of such a statement suggests the absence of this happy condition.

Analyzing supplier breadth is harder. Annual reports dance around the topic. They rarely state how much of total costs went to their biggest vendor. So it's often best to just think about what a business needs to buy. Must inventory be a certain brand, or will any do? Do key components come from a country where one family controls commerce, or are they available globally? Are qualified workers scarce and unionized, or plentiful and easily trained?

Sometimes the illusion of a broad supplier base is dangled in front of the investor. For example, a 10-K might state that a company "sources from over 100 suppliers." Don't read into such statements. A business with 100 vendors could still make over half of its purchases from just one of them.

Breadth analysis weeds out dicey situations quickly. In early 2007, I looked at Delta Financial Corporation, a consumer mortgage lender based in New York. The company helped people with bad credit records buy homes, and did so in a way that seemed to me to be satisfactorily cautious. I understood it, and was satisfied with its historic operating performance.

Once Delta originated a mortgage, it *securitized* it. It sold the loan on the residential mortgage-backed securities market, and used the proceeds to make other loans. I viewed the company's product as *money*, and the buyers of these loans as its *suppliers*. There were many buyers, so the supplier base at first glance seemed to be broad.[1]

But then I started to see the residential mortgage-backed securities market *itself* as the supplier. It was newly huge, and a key conduit in the process. Any interruption in its functioning could create trouble for Delta. So I passed.

Note that I wasn't forecasting interest rates, calculating default percentages, or doing anything else fancy. I just noticed that the company seemed overly dependent on what amounted to a single supplier. When the financial crisis started some months later, the residential mortgage-backed securities market did in fact seize up. No longer able to securitize mortgages, Delta filed for bankruptcy.[2]

I'm rarely this accurate in predicting why something will explode. Delta was unusual in that respect. But it was typical in that a precarious circumstance was spotted through the blunt yet reliable tool of breadth analysis.

A second qualitative tool is *forces analysis*. It's my cheap rendition of the five forces model introduced by business school professor Michael E. Porter in 1979.[3]

Porter's original model gauges the intensity of competition within an *industry*, and the resulting profitability of firms in that industry. My version uses four of those forces to estimate profit prospects for a *company*. One decides whether each force is strong or weak. The weaker the forces, the more profitable the company.

Porter measures profitability with *return on invested capital*, or *ROIC*. The way he calculates it makes it nearly identical to my preferred profitability metric, ROCE.

The first force is the *bargaining power of customers*. If a company's clients demanded lower prices or faster delivery times, would they get them?

Three things can lower customer bargaining power. One is the number of customers. The more there are, the lower their power. If breadth analysis revealed a sustainably broad customer base, customer bargaining power is probably weak.

Another is the improbability of *backward integration*. When a customer backward integrates, it starts doing something previously done by the company. If it can't—because it would need a competence far away from its core activity, for example—its bargaining power is weaker.

A third is high *switching costs*. If a customer would incur large expenses by switching to one of the company's competitors—because its operations are tightly integrated into those of the company, for example—customer bargaining power is weaker.

West Marine, an American retailer of boating accessories, provides an example. I analyzed the company in 2011 following the demise of its largest competitor.[4] What I found was that boaters were effectively demanding lower prices based on offers from other retailers online. Worse, some were *showrooming*, or refining their product choices in West Marine branches and then buying from cheaper Internet-only stores. This hurt West Marine's profitability as it was forced to offer discounts.

Boaters are unlikely to backward integrate by making their own life preservers and outboard motors, of course. But they have low switching costs, and there are plenty of other places to shop for accessories. So the bargaining power of the company's customers is strong. Unsurprisingly, West Marine's stock price hasn't risen since I first looked at it five years ago.

Contrast this with International Flavors & Fragrances. It produces proprietary compounds that give branded foods and soaps their signature tastes and smells. Once a food or soap manufacturer has specified an International compound into a formula, the manufacturer's customers come to expect the sensation it delivers. This gives International the ability to raise prices over time, as demonstrated by its consistent profitability.[5] Compared to West Marine, the bargaining power of International's customers is weak.

The second force is the *bargaining power of suppliers*. If suppliers hiked prices or demanded faster payment, would the company give in?

The things that lower supplier bargaining power echo the things that lower customer bargaining power. One is the number of suppliers.

More means weaker. If breadth analysis revealed a sustainably broad supplier base, supplier bargaining power is probably weak.

Another is the improbability of *forward integration*. When a vendor forward integrates, it starts doing something previously done by the company. The less conceivable this scenario, the weaker suppliers' bargaining power.

A third is low switching costs. The less expensive it is for the company to change vendors, the weaker supplier bargaining power is.

Consider the Kraft Heinz Company. Kraft Heinz is the American producer of Grey Poupon mustard, Jell-O desserts, and other supermarket staples. It makes these products out of commodities— milk, sugar, tomatoes—which it can buy from a broad base of global suppliers.[6] If one supplier is unable to meet the company's delivery schedule or cost requirements, Kraft Heinz can turn to another. There are many. The company's positive operating income comes in part from the weak bargaining power of its suppliers.

The third force is the *threat of substitutes*. Substitutes take three forms. One is *direct substitutes*, or similar products offered by existing competitors. Two is *doing without*, a concept from economics. Three is *wholly different* products that perform the same basic function.

Consider Axis, a Swedish company that produces digital video surveillance cameras. Direct substitutes for Axis's products are digital video surveillance cameras from Panasonic, Samsung, and other competitors.

*Doing without* could mean sticking with old technology like analog video surveillance cameras. Or it could mean forgoing electronic security systems altogether. This could follow a rational choice to accept the cost of theft from unsecured premises instead of paying more for a digital video surveillance system.

*Wholly different* products that perform the same basic function would include a fence, a guard service, and nonvideo security devices like heat sensors.[7]

Two things can keep the threat of substitutes low. One is if the substitutes offer lower value than do the company's offerings. Another is if the company's customers would incur high switching costs by adopting substitutes.

The fourth force is the *threat of new entrants*. New entrants come in the form of both start-ups and new divisions of existing companies.

The less likely it is that new entrants will emerge, the weaker the threat they pose.

The threat of new entrants is different from *barriers to entry*. It's barriers to entry plus what I call *barriers to success*. Both have to be there to constitute a strong threat. A new entrant that easily initiates operations but has no chance of meaningfully penetrating a market isn't much of a threat.

A company may have attributes that keep potential new entrants on the sidelines. One is economies of scale. The company's production volume may result in lower per-unit costs than those of a newcomer. Another is high customer switching costs, which make a new player's offerings expensive to try. Last is hard-to-get permits, if the company is in a regulated industry. Just one of these three attributes can dull the threat of new entrants.

To effectively use forces analysis, one must make decisions. One must call each force as either strong or weak. *Medium* isn't useful. After all, they're *all* kind of medium. Just determine whether each force is more on the strong side of things, or more on the weak side of things.

If all four forces acting on a company are weak, further consideration of the investment is warranted. If two or more are strong, the opposite is true. One should stop. Between those extremes lies a multitude of competitive situations that require judgment of the sort that gets easier with experience. When in doubt, quit the analysis and find another company to look at.

I quit often. In early 2015 I analyzed GameStop, a leading chain of video game stores. One force that gave me pause was the bargaining power of suppliers. Three video game publishers—Sony, Microsoft, and Nintendo—each accounted for over 10 percent of GameStop's new inventory purchases during 2014. And no wonder. When one of these publishers came out with a new release, GameStop *had* to stock it.[8] This gave its vendors strong bargaining power.

Another force that concerned me was the threat of substitutes. While many new video games were still being sold in physical form in stores, an increasing number were being sold in digital form online. Of course GameStop operated websites that competed in this virtual space. But the trend evidenced how potent a substitute downloads were to the company's core physical operation.

Since GameStop faced at least two strong forces, I considered it no further. It's been less than two years since that analysis—hardly long enough to cite the market as validation—but the stock price has dropped.

Porter's original five forces model is great. Many good investors use it unmodified. But because it's designed to analyze an industry instead of a company, I prefer my tweaked version. Whichever one prefers, some framework for assessing competitive forces is key in forecasting a company's future profitability.

A third qualitative tool is what I call *moat identification*. A moat is a barrier that protects a business from competition. It's a defense that lasts.

Most businesses don't have a moat. They're rare. Discovering a business with strong historic operating metrics that's also protected by a moat is an infrequent event.

If a company does have a moat, that moat has a *source*. A *single, identified* source. There are six potential sources.

The first is *government*. Governments grant special rights to some companies. Consider Weyerhaeuser, a timberland REIT based near Seattle. One of Weyerhauser's businesses is managing 14 million acres of forest in Canada.

These aren't forests that Weyerhauser *owns*, they're forests that Weyerhauser *manages*. Each is owned by the Canadian province in which it's located. So it's the provincial governments that grant forest management licenses to Weyerhauser.

These licenses are valuable. They give Weyerhauser the exclusive right to cut down trees and sell them. Each license lasts for between 15 and 25 years and is renewable.[9] If a competing company wanted to manage these forests, it would have to wait a long time just to apply. Weyerhauser is protected, owing to a moat sourced from government.

A second source of moat is *network*. Network is an accumulation of users or customers. It constitutes a moat if it yields a product benefit derived from the other users of a product.

Consider Facebook, the website based near San Francisco. People join Facebook to stay in touch with friends, share photos, and stay connected to people that they like. As they build their collection of contacts, they become increasingly *locked in* to Facebook. If they leave, they lose a means of communicating with others. This gives

Facebook a reliable stream of page views, which the company sells to advertisers.[10]

Launching a rival social network would not be technically difficult. But prying Facebook's users away from the online circles of friends that they've built would be tough.

A third source of moat is *cost*. Sometimes a company has a *low cost structure* that enables it to produce a product for less than competitors. A low cost structure may come from a proprietary manufacturing technology, an inexpensive operating method, or some quirk of history. Take POSCO, the South Korean steel manufacturer. POSCO was created by the Korean government in the 1960s when it decided that the country needed a domestic steel maker.[11]

Korea launched the new enterprise by giving it land on which to build steel factories. *Gave*. And not just any land. It was located along a deepwater shoreline, which enabled POSCO to receive shipments of iron ore and coal—the key raw materials in steel manufacturing—without having to pay any inland transportation costs.[12]

Compare this lucky history with that of U.S. Steel, the largest steel manufacturer in the United States. U.S. Steel had to buy its land. No matter what U.S. Steel does, it can't match the cost advantage POSCO has from its seaside industrial property. Not surprisingly, POSCO is recognized for having one of the lowest manufacturing costs per ton in the steel industry.[13]

A fourth source of moat is *brand*. Some brands are so strong that customers rarely consider substitutes. An example is the instant noodle business of Nestlé, the food manufacturer based in Switzerland. Nestlé's brand in this category is Maggi.[14] In India, where instant noodles are particularly popular, Maggi has over half of the market. That's a tremendous share. In fact, the Maggi name is so accepted in India that many people there don't say "instant noodles." They say "Maggi." That's strong evidence of a brand formidable enough to keep many would-be competitors away.[15]

Identifying a moat that comes from brand can be harder than identifying one that comes from government, network, or cost. Brand is a softer, more nuanced characteristic. Gauging its strength is easiest to someone in the target market.

Citizens of India appreciate the strength of the Maggi name. But an investor with no ties to the country could miss it. Maggi's dominant market share—which an investor unconnected to India *could* identify—doesn't indicate a moat by itself. After all, that could come from promotional pricing. So how do far-away investors know if there's a brand-based moat?

By talking to people in the target market. They avoid saying the brand name, and see what gets mentioned. They use *unaided recall* questions like "What's your favorite instant noodle?"

Admittedly, a Palo Alto investor researching Nestlé has no trouble finding people in Maggi's target market. The area has many immigrants from India. I had only to ask friends on my soccer team. But through acquaintances and social networks, the enterprising investor can often reach people in any target market.

A fifth source of moat is *switching costs*. High switching costs have a powerful retention effect on customers. Consider Oracle, the database software company based near San Francisco.[16] Oracle customers store years' worth of data on the company's systems, and integrate those systems deeply within their operations. A company migrating to another database software solution would need to buy new hardware, retrain employees, incur downtime, and reintegrate entire processes. The resulting expense would be high, dissuading many customers from changing vendors.[17]

A sixth source of moat is what I call *ingrainedness*. It's like brand, but it applies to the channel instead of the end user. A company enjoys ingrainedness when it's so integral to a value chain that it's difficult to picture its industry without it.

Take Geberit, a Swiss manufacturer of plumbing components. Launched in 1905, the company does several things to embed itself into the practices of professional plumbers. It provides training and certifications. It distributes free project planning software that specifies Geberit components automatically. Programs like these have embedded the company's offerings so deeply into the operations of its channel partners that competitors face serious challenges trying to steal market share.[18]

Like brand, ingrainedness can be hard for someone outside of the channel to see. Unless one is a European plumber, Geberit may be invisible. So again, astute investors talk to people in the channel. They ask open-ended questions to see if the name of a favored firm comes up.

One rarely does. Again, when it comes to moats, *most businesses don't have one.*

A fourth qualitative tool is *market growth assessment.* This is a straightforward view on whether a company's market is growing or not. It's important because a business with an expanding market—everything else being equal—has a brighter future than one that doesn't.

Exact percentage growth rates are neither required nor useful. A basic sense that demand for a company's products is increasing is sufficient. This can be based on an elementary belief that the population is growing.

Projecting growth well requires some restraint. Because the investment idea has already passed through several stages of the model by this point, it may be developing a bit of a glow to the investor. Market growth assessment provides a ready stage for this enthusiasm. The antidote is to simply remain realistic and not get carried away with upward-sloping curves.

There's some obvious overlap between the four qualitative tools. Supplier breadth analysis, for example, feels a lot like the bargaining power of suppliers. Moat identification draws heavily on the threat of substitutes. But some redundancy is helpful. It lessens the chance that an important factor will be missed.

As the four tools make clear, qualitative forecasting is my preferred way to assess a company's prospects. But many prefer *quantitative* forecasting. This involves using spreadsheets to calculate expected revenues, margins, interest rates, and the like. It's the dummying-up of future period financial statements. I don't like this approach, for two reasons.

First, it's hard. Making predictions about prices, costs, and market shares is just plain difficult. It often devolves to nothing more than guesswork cloaked in mathematics.

Second, it can be self-deceiving. Those dummied-up statements look *awfully official.* They create the risk that one will mistake precision for accuracy. The truth is that one can't know exactly how tomorrow's financials will look. But if one owns parts of businesses with both good operating histories and solid strategic positionings, it's likely that the future will play out well.

## Summary

Assess a company's prospects with four qualitative tools:

1. Breadth analysis
2. Forces analysis
3. Moat identification
4. Market growth assessment

Forces analysis involves assessing each of the following four forces as either strong or weak:

1. Bargaining power of customers
2. Bargaining power of suppliers
3. Threat of substitutes
4. Threat of new entrants

Moats, which are rare, come from one of six sources:

1. Government
2. Cost
3. Brand
4. Network
5. Switching costs
6. Ingrainedness

---

### CASE STUDY

### Kone Oyj

Kone makes and services elevators and escalators. Based in Finland, it's one of the five largest companies in its industry. Most of its sales are in Asia and Europe, with over a third coming from China alone.

Kone's historic operating metrics are remarkable. Even with conservative assumptions, ROCE has averaged over 20 percent, and ΔFCF/FDS has averaged over 10 percent. Strategic analysis helps to determine if such outperformance can continue:

http://www.goodstockscheap.com/12.1.htm

First is breadth analysis. Regarding customers, the company's annual report states "Kone's customer base consists of a large number of customers in several market areas, with no individual customer representing a material share of Kone's sales."

This isn't the ideal statement, as it doesn't define *material* as 10 percent or more. But it's adequate. One can safely conclude that the customer base is acceptably fragmented.

Could the customer base consolidate? Unlikely. Building owners don't seem poised to go through some sort of global consolidation frenzy.

Is the supplier base broad? Here the annual report offers even less ideal statements, like "a significant part of Kone's component suppliers and global supply capacity is located in China."

So, as usual, one must think about the things that Kone needs to buy. It's helpful to divide the business into two parts: goods and services.

The goods are elevators, escalators, and parts. What Kone needs to buy here is commodity materials like rubber, glass, and steel; and the services of subcontractors to make components. Commodity materials come from many sources. And while some subcontractors are better than others, it's likely that many potential subcontractors exist.

The services are maintaining and fixing elevators and escalators. Here, what Kone needs to buy is labor. How tight is the labor pool? Becoming an elevator service technician clearly requires some training. But it's not like becoming a medical doctor. Total training time is likely to take months or a year, not a decade or more. In other words, the size of Kone's service labor pool can be readily grown.

Is the labor unionized? In much of the world, yes. But it's not like airline pilots that are both unionized *and* require years of training. So while the service supplier base isn't ideal from the perspective of an outside investor, it's just broad enough, and just unlikely to consolidate enough, to be satisfactory. On balance, breadth analysis gives Kone a clean bill of health.

It's probably already clear that I rooted around for information beyond that provided in Kone's annual report. But my sources are available to anyone. I'll detail them shortly.

The second tool is forces analysis. It's again useful to think of Kone in two parts, goods and services. Start with goods.

First is the bargaining power of customers. Breadth analysis made clear that there were many customers. Plus, they're unlikely to backward integrate. Building owners and property developers don't go into the elevator manufacturing business, because so doing would require a very different set of competencies than does managing a skyscraper or developing real estate. To be sure, capital equipment sales is competitive. But on balance, the bargaining power of Kone's goods customers is weak.

Next is the bargaining power of suppliers. Breadth analysis found that the supplier base was sustainably fragmented. In addition, it's hard to picture a glass maker or a component subcontractor forward integrating into the escalator business. Plus, Kone can change suppliers without incurring significant switching costs. As evidence, the annual report notes that Kone focuses on developing "readiness for transferring the manufacturing of critical components from one production line or supplier to another." The bargaining power of Kone's goods suppliers is therefore weak.

Next is the threat of substitutes. A potential goods customer could easily choose a competitor. A property developer or building owner can buy a new elevator or escalator from any of several global leaders. The largest are Otis, Schindler, and ThyssenKrupp.

The two other manifestations of substitute threat don't apply in the Kone case. Exploring why is illuminating. *Doing without* means stairs. But tall buildings need an efficient way for people to reach the higher floors. Even if all the occupants were springy athletes, laws like the Americans with Disabilities Act would still require elevators in most cases.[19] As for *wholly different* products that perform the same basic function, there aren't any besides maybe helicopters or scaffolding. Neither is practical enough to rise to the level of *threat*.

But the direct substitute threat—from Otis, Schindler, and ThyssenKrupp—is real. Therefore, the threat of substitutes on the goods side is strong.

Last is the threat of new entrants. When something goes wrong with an elevator, it can go *very wrong*. Sudden stops cause back injuries. Doors not opening cause panic attacks. Falls into shaftways cause death. These prospects bias building owners and developers against unknown entrants. A rookie firm would have to fight against established brands that enjoy reputations for safety. This makes the threat of new entrants weak.

One might ask, what about General Electric? It's a trusted industrial name. What if GE decided to get into the elevator business? Or Germany's Siemens, for that matter?

*Touché.* My claim that a newcomer would be handicapped is very much my *opinion*. To me, a new elevator provider would face a bigger challenge than, say, a new brand of potato chip, where the perceived cost of failure is lower.

*But it's all opinion.* The threat of new entrants, the discount rate used to capitalize operating leases, the appropriateness of director compensation—all reflect one's judgments. Subjectivity is inescapable. That's investing.

Turning to Kone's service business, start with the bargaining power of customers. Most new Kone equipment comes with a year of maintenance. So for the first 12 months, there's little incentive for a customer to consider outside service outfits. After that, the vast majority of customers sign a commercial maintenance contract with Kone. When those expire, most renew.

It's easy to see why Kone equipment customers prefer Kone services. For one, the company may have more timely technical knowledge about its own products than would independent service providers. In addition, Kone may have preferential access to proprietary replacement parts. That's why the bargaining power of Kone's service customers is weak.

Consider now the bargaining power of suppliers. Breadth analysis showed a sustainably fragmented supplier base. And while forward integration is conceivable—service technicians can leave Kone and start their own repair shops—it's not imminent *en masse*. Also, Kone faces low switching costs in replacing a departing service technician. It may lose the benefit of some sunk training costs, but it can switch without material penalty. For these reasons the bargaining power of Kone's service suppliers—labor—is weak.

Next is the threat of substitutes. Some Kone equipment customers do use independent service providers. But a year of services is included with new equipment. That limits the threat of direct substitutes for a time. Then, the renewal rate is high. This limits the threat of direct substitutes for the duration of the new maintenance contract. Indeed, the threat of direct substitutes is real only during seams between contract periods.

As for the other kinds of substitute threats, *doing without* is in most cases illegal. Governments mandate elevator maintenance. For example in California, the Department of Industrial Relations requires annual elevator inspections.[20] Deferred maintenance causes inspection failures, which can effectively suspend building use. As for *wholly different* products that perform the same basic function, there aren't any. So the threat of service substitutes is weak.

Last is the threat of new entrants. Skilled technicians can start a local service outfit with little capital and a handful of customers. So the barriers to entry are not high. Neither are the barriers to success. Small servicers can develop good reputations in their communities. In fact, Kone routinely buys such start-ups. It made 23 acquisitions in 2015, and 17 the year before. Most were of regional maintenance firms.[21] This pattern of acquisitions proves that the threat of new entrants is strong, at least on a market-by-market basis.

How does forces analysis gauge Kone overall? With goods, there was only one strong force: the threat of substitutes. Specifically, the threat of *direct* substitutes from competitors like Otis. This likely manifests itself in intense bidding competitions for new equipment sales. But the other three forces are all weak.

On the services side, the only strong force was the threat of new entrants. But this threat seems limited to local markets, and again, the other three forces are weak. So to the astute investor, Kone continues to look good.

The third tool is moat identification. Consider Kone's goods business. Many parts of a Kone elevator or escalator are proprietary. Replacing a part therefore often requires buying something from Kone, either directly or indirectly through a local servicer.

Now look at Kone's service business. It enjoys advantages over competitors through superior technical knowledge and proprietary parts access. That's why its renewal rates are so high.

These factors all point toward a moat sourced from *switching costs*. For a Kone equipment owner to no longer buy from Kone at all would require ripping out an elevator or escalator and replacing it with one from a different maker. That's expensive.

At first, government may also seem to be a moat source for Kone. This is because government agencies require elevator maintenance. But they don't specify what firm has to provide the maintenance in the way that the Canadian provinces specify Weyerhauser as the manager of their timberlands.

But even without government as a source, Kone has a moat. It comes from switching costs.

The fourth tool is market growth assessment. A belief that the population will continue to grow is probably enough to conclude that Kone's market will expand satisfactorily. But two other dynamics suggest that it may grow even more.

One is urbanization. People are moving to cities. Land in the city is more expensive than land in the country. This motivates property developers to build taller buildings. More tall buildings means more elevators and escalators.

Another is aging. People are living longer lives. Because climbing stairs gets harder with age, they are spending more years in single-floor condominiums rather than in two- or three-story houses. For both of these reasons, Kone's market growth potential seems healthy.

On balance, the four tools of qualitative analysis make Kone look good. The company's strong historic operating performance is likely to sustain. The astute investor continues to put Kone through the value investing model.

My sole role with elevators is *passenger*. I've never bought one, recommended one, fixed one, or replaced one. I'm about as outside of Kone's target market as one can get. And yet the four qualitative tools called on me to secure some insights. To do so, I drew on two resources.

First was Kone's investor relations department. I e-mailed them questions. What percentage of their new equipment sales came with service contracts? How long were those contracts? Was labor unionized? Questions with factual answers are the best sort to ask of investor relations departments.

Chapter 2 noted that investor relations departments range from helpful to unresponsive. Kone's was exemplary. It spoiled me with its speed and thoroughness. This no doubt colored my view of the company, as it should. As noted, *how* an investor relations department responds *is part of the answer*.

The other resource was people in the target market. For example, I called the person in charge of elevator maintenance at a California organization that owns several buildings. I explained to him that I was researching an elevator investment, knew nothing about elevators, knew that he did, and would be grateful for his views. For this candor I got a torrent of information and opinions that no brokerage report could ever provide.

People crave being listened to. That's why a thirst for listening is among the investor's most valuable tools. With that thirst, the only thing that separates one from insight is time.

## CHAPTER 13

# Shareholder-Friendliness

Do I understand it? → Is it good?

Products
Customers
Industry
Form
Geography
Status

Past
  ROCE
  FCFROCE
  ΔOI/FDS
  ΔFCF/FDS
  ΔBV/FDS
  ΔTDV/FDS
  Liabilities-to-equity

Future
  Breadth analysis
  Forces analysis
  Moat identification
  Market growth

Shareholder-friendliness
  Compensation & ownership
  Related-party transactions
  Share repurchases
  Dividends

If a business has been historically good based on performance metrics, and promises to remain good based on strategic analysis, then it's on its way to registering as good overall. The final checkpoint is to see if the company is *shareholder-friendly.*

A shareholder-friendly company works primarily for the benefit of its outside owners. It sends—in one form or another—its free cash flow to its investors. Gauging shareholder-friendliness is a qualitative procedure based on four indicators.

There are no fixed benchmarks for these indicators. There are no thresholds that, if crossed, put a company squarely in the shareholder-friendly camp. Instead, the indicators must be considered together to make a judgment of the sort that gets more reliable with practice.

The first indicator is *compensation and ownership*. What executives and board members earn and own shapes their incentives. We'd like these incentives to be as aligned with ours as possible.

In the ideal situation, executives earn a reasonable salary. Board members are paid normal fees for their part-time jobs. And they all used their *own cash* to purchase shares in the company at *market prices* such that their holdings constitute the *bulk* of their net worths.

Alas, reality departs from this paradigm in several ways. For one, salaries are often gargantuan. Eight-figure pay packages are common, particularly in America. Also, annual directors' fees regularly approach the mid six-figures.

In addition, stock option plans are commonplace. These schemes allow for shares to be purchased at the low price of an earlier year, and then sold right away. This lets officers and directors participate in the upside of equity ownership without exposure to the corresponding downside. Such automatic gain arrangements hardly represent an equal yoking with investors. Any suggestion that they align incentives is laughable.

Even if an insider purchased stock at market prices, it's hard to know how big a part of that person's portfolio the investment is. A CEO with 50 percent of net worth tied up in the company is more likely to act in the interest of shareholders than one with just 5 percent. But gauging portfolio weight is rarely possible.

In most countries officer compensation must be disclosed. It appears either in the annual report, or in a referenced document such as a *proxy statement*. Unfortunately, it's often fluffed up to mountains of unmanageable text. A full third of a 50-page American proxy statement might dwell on management pay.

A useful shortcut is to search for the *summary compensation table*. This concise presentation lays plain the total paid to each executive for each of the last three years. The far-right column lumps together each officer's salary, bonus, and stock-based consideration

Disclosed and approved are different. Neither auditors nor government agencies certify the appropriateness of compensation packages. That's for the investor to do.

I focus on the *total* amount that went to the *highest paid* employee. I don't care how much of it was salary, how much of it was bonus, and how much of it was stock. I know that compensation packages are routinely dressed up to look like cheese at the end of a mouse maze. That's why I just want the fattest, hairiest number.

I gauge this number with floating guidelines. My current standard is if it's over $30,000,000, or over 5 percent of the lower of free cash flow or net income, I'm not interested. What revenue was doesn't matter. An executive's house size needn't increase in lockstep with sales.

Also disclosed are fees paid to members of the board. Search the proxy statement for the term *director compensation*. I look for the amount that went to the highest paid outside director. *Outside* means not also a full-time company employee. This is often the *non-executive chair* or the *lead independent director.*

Currently I like to see the highest paid outside director get total annual consideration of around $250,000. I stop my analysis if it's more than twice that.

These standards—$30,000,000 for an executive, $500,000 for a director—are very American. Both numbers would be absurdly high in most other countries. In Norway, for example, it's common for directors of large public companies to receive less than $100,000 per year. So fees must be considered in context.

The link between compensation and long-term shareholder return is not obvious. Outrageous pay packages have become so normal, and so institutionally reinforced, that they infect outperforming and laggard companies alike.

In addition, officer compensation can be just a sliver of a company's overall expenses. Whether a chief executive makes $5,000,000 or $10,000,000 has little direct mathematical impact on a company with $1,000,000,000 in income. At the earnings-per-share level, the difference is undetectable. So why do we care?

We care because compensation offers a rare window into the decision-making processes at the highest levels of a company. Executives and directors that approve outsized pay are prone to other aggrandizements. They're more likely to consent to overpriced acquisitions, for example. Why? Because they're less willing to jeopardize their own remunerative posts by opposing an acquisition championed by a colleague.

Talented business people should be amply rewarded for their work. But excessive compensation is a dangerous enabler. Its follow-on effects hurt outside shareholders. Paying too much for management may be bearable by itself, but paying too much for acquisitions can kill companies. That's why I favor teams that are properly paid. This preference causes me to miss some opportunities. But it keeps me clear of more catastrophes. That's my kind of trade-off.

Also shaping incentives is ownership. Significant, outright holdings by executives and directors of stock in the company they steward is a positive sign.

It's easy to find out how much of a company is owned by insiders. Search the 10-K or proxy statement for the term *beneficial*. A chart will appear with a clumsy title like *security ownership of management and certain beneficial owners*. Consider only owners that also serve as executives and directors of the company. Investment firms—which are on the chart if they own over a certain percentage of the stock—should be ignored. They're not the ones running the company.

Outside of the United States, search the annual report for the term *shareholder* or *ownership*.

Material insider buying at market prices is also a promising indicator. This is reliably revealed in the *insider transactions* sections of financial websites. Note that a *non–open market* acquisition generally indicates the exercise of an option. This doesn't point toward shareholder-friendliness by itself. It's the *open market* purchases that are positives.

Insider stock *sales* are never positive, but may not be negative either. Directors may need cash to pay for a child's college tuition. Executives may want to pay off mortgages. Founders that own most of their companies may sell a bit each month as part of personal financial plans. These are all legitimate reasons to sell. Of course if several insiders dump most of their shares at once, that's bad. But routine dispositions aren't as conclusive.

A second indicator of shareholder-friendliness is *related-party transactions*. A party is *related* if it has dealings with the company that could pose a conflict of interest. A vendor to the company that's owned by a company board member would be an example of such a party.

Related-party transactions aren't necessarily bad. They're fine if negotiated at *arm's length*. Arm's length is the metaphorical distance that restricts purchases to what's truly needed and holds prices to market rates.

As a general rule, the number and size of such dealings, as well as the opacity in disclosure, are inversely correlated with shareholder-friendliness. If there's just one or two small related-party transactions, and the detail offered on them is extensive, they're less likely to hurt the outside investor.

Related-party transactions are easy to find. Search the proxy statement for the term *related* or *relationships*. What comes up will commonly involve leasing, consulting, or hiring.

Consider leasing. Sometimes an executive or director will own, directly or indirectly, an entity that rents real estate to the company. For example, retailer H&M rents some of its stores from entities owned by its chairman. The company's annual report states that in 2015 such leases totaled 436,000,000 Swedish kronor,[1] or about $52,000,000.

That's a lot of money. Does it reflect market rates? It's hard to know. How big were the stores? That detail isn't given. But the report does offer the physical addresses of each property. That's good disclosure.

One blunt test for fairness is to see how much of a company's total lease expenses went to the insider entity. H&M's annual report says that rent expenses in 2015 totaled 20,554,000,000 Swedish kronor.[2] Some quick math reveals that the chairman's entity got only 2 percent of that. So supporting an insider's real estate holdings clearly isn't a primary function of H&M. That finding, plus the address disclosure, makes this setup seem less troubling.

Another type of related-party transaction involves consulting. Sometimes a director will be paid to provide special advisory services to the company. Take Costco, a retailer based near Seattle. In 2015 it paid a member of its board $300,000 to consult.[3] Was that too much? How many hours did he work? Few details are given. That by itself is a negative. But sometimes the best thing to do is to file a fact away, and judge it later in the context of other, less ambiguous shareholder-friendliness indicators.

A third type of potentially questionable dealing involves hiring. Sometimes a company job goes to a member of an insider's family. Officerships may pass from one generation to the next. The current head of H&M is the grandson of the founder.[4] At Los Angeles entertainment company Twenty-First Century Fox, two senior executives are sons of the former chairman.[5] Across the country at envelope manufacturer Cenveo, two top officers are also sons of the chairman.[6] Are these bad?

Views on this tend to vary by country. In Sweden, management dynasties are seen as sorts of benevolent monarchies. They're thought to further the long-term prospects of companies in ways that guns-for-hire never could. This surprises many Americans, who see dynasties as undermining meritocracy. They just can't believe that the best qualified person for the job happened to spring from the loins of the predecessor.

I personally view management dynasties as questionable, but not disqualifying. If they're unhealthy, that fact tends to show up elsewhere. It may drive ROCE down, or executive compensation up. Bad managers cause bad outcomes, whatever families they come from. So I stay alert for the sour results of nepotism without assuming that managers with familiar last names are dopes.

Virtually all related-party transaction disclosures come with some assurance of fairness. *This was purchased in the ordinary course of business at market rates*, for example.

Such phrases can be unconvincing. After all, they're thin on details. We don't know the size of the stores, the number of hours worked, or the IQ of the offspring. But that's okay. We don't need to know everything. We just want to avoid *blatant plunderage*. We want a basic sense that there aren't undeserved bonuses masquerading as something else.

In some countries the definition of *related party* is unnecessarily broad. It can, for example, include subsidiaries. We needn't consider transactions between a company and its subsidiaries. They're normal, and don't threaten to pose a conflict of interest in the way that transactions with insider-owned entities do.

A third indicator of shareholder-friendliness is *share repurchases.* Many investors view companies buying their own stock back in the open market as positive. They may be. But only if the shares are bought at a discount to value.

Bargain buybacks are delightful in all respects. They're the kind of price-below-worth investments we'd make ourselves. Plus, they're tax efficient. When a company increases income per share by decreasing the denominator, it pays us in an untaxed way. The stock price is urged to rise, owing to a drop in the number of claimants on the company's earnings. Compare this to dividends, which—depending on where they're paid and received—are usually taxed as income.

But repurchases at other-than-discount prices aren't useful to the outside investor. They're as destructive as overpriced acquisitions. Indeed, they effectively *are* overpriced acquisitions.

Alas, managements may be motivated to repurchase even without a discount. This is because of incentive compensation plans. Some bonuses kick in when earnings per share rise. By using free cash flow to purchase stock on the open market, executives can juice earnings per share *even if total income doesn't increase.*

Stock option plans exacerbate this. To the extent that the market prices stocks at some multiple of earnings per share, buybacks cause share prices to rise, making it profitable for executives to exercise options and immediately sell.

Accounting facilitates this game. Stock repurchases show up on the balance sheet. Cash decreases on the assets side, and equity decreases by an equal amount. Repurchases also register on the cash flow statement. They're a cash outflow from financing. But they're absent from the income statement. No expense is recognized. In other words, accounting has no way to call out overpayments at the time that they're made.

This is why buybacks also have the short-term effect of turbo-charging ROCE. The denominator drops, but the numerator doesn't.

Buybacks are disclosed in annual reports and 10-Ks. Search for the term *repurchase.*

A commonly cited justification for buybacks is that they coun-terbalance the issuance of options under a stock option plan. By repurchasing shares while new options are granted, the number of fully diluted shares can be made to stay roughly the same.

I hereby nominate this as one of the worst rationales in the history of finance. Using company cash to transfer shares from outsiders to insiders has a name. *Theft.* The only good reason to buy back shares is because they're inexpensive relative to their worth. In the next chapter we'll see how to gauge that worth.

The fourth indicator is *dividends.* Many investors regard meaningful dividends as a hallmark of a shareholder-friendly company. And they may be. But dividends have some drawbacks.

First, as noted earlier, they're taxable. And because the issuer picks the timing and size of dividends, the tax liability hits shareholders on a schedule that they don't control. This contrasts with buybacks, where the profitable sale of stock made possible by increasing earnings per share can happen at a time more of the shareholder's choosing. For example, an investor can decide to realize a gain during an otherwise low income year to enjoy a lower tax bracket. Or the investor can sell while living in a low-tax jurisdiction. Dividends offer no such time-shifting.

Another problem with dividends is that they may signal that a company has no growth opportunities. A firm with the chance to deploy capital in high-rate-of-return activities would logically plow the bulk of its earnings back into the business. If it doesn't, maybe it can't. Perhaps its high return possibilities are all tapped out.

This notion often comes up with companies in flashy industries. It's alleged to be why they *don't* pay dividends. The internal growth opportunities, they say, are *just too good.* Silicon Valley is *lined* with non–dividend payers.

I consider dividends most shareholder-friendly when they're paid by fully priced companies in mature industries with long histories of strong free cash flow.

It may seem odd to think of dividends as a *qualitative* characteristic. After all, they're numbers. *Dividend yield*—annual dividends divided by current stock price—is an oft-quoted statistic. But dividends represent a use of cash for which there are alternatives. Shares could be repurchased, growth capex could be increased, and other businesses could be bought. So dividends are best viewed as one piece of the shareholder-friendliness puzzle. Boiling them down to a percentage is an oversimplification.

Dividend practices vary around the world. In Europe, it's common for companies to regularly pay out a preannounced percentage of their income as dividends. That's less common in America, where dividends are more discretionary.

Laws also matter. In Germany, for example, only profitable companies can pay dividends.[7] Contrast this with the United States, where some loss-making firms go as far as to borrow money to maintain their dividend. A company's dividend practices must therefore be weighed in the context of varying customs, expectations, and regulations around the world.

Viewed comprehensively, the four indicators give a dependable view of shareholder-friendliness. A company that pays no dividend, buys back shares only during price slumps, and is run by modestly compensated executives that collectively own a third of the company is shareholder-friendly. One that repurchases stock too expensively, pays each outside director $600,000 per year, and leases the bulk of its office space from a trust benefiting the founder's family isn't. Scattered around these examples are variants that get easier to assess with experience.

## Summary

Gauging shareholder-friendliness is a qualitative process based on four indicators:

1. Compensation and ownership
2. Related-party transactions
3. Share repurchases
4. Dividends

---

**CASE STUDY**

## The Swatch Group SA and Fossil Group, Inc.

Swatch is the largest watchmaker in the world by revenue. Based in Switzerland, it owns well-known brands like Longines, Omega, and its namesake:

> http://www.goodstockscheap.com/13.1.htm

Fossil is another leading watchmaker. It's based in Texas:

> http://www.goodstockscheap.com/13.2.htm

> http://www.goodstockscheap.com/13.3.htm

These two companies have different shareholder-friendliness profiles, as evidenced by the four indicators.

First consider compensation and ownership. Swatch's highest paid officer in 2015 was its CEO. He made 6,878,700 Swiss francs,[8] which is about equal to the same amount in U.S. dollars. That's above the Swiss national average, but not above the American.

The highest paid director was the chairwoman, who made 4,421,951 Swiss francs.[9] But at Swatch that's a full-time executive position. What's more relevant is what the highest paid *outside* director made. That number was 174,996 Swiss francs,[10] which again is about equal to the same amount in U.S. dollars. That's fine.

Regarding ownership, Swatch's annual report states that at the end of 2015, executives and directors collectively owned 56,709,793 registered shares and 2,800 bearer shares.[11]

The two share classes make interpreting this a little complicated. The key fact is that bearer shares have five times the economic interest of registered shares. That is, if in one year earnings per bearer share is 20, earnings per registered share is 4. So executives and directors collectively own the economic equivalent of 11,344,759 bearer shares. That's just the quantity 56,709,793 divided by five, plus 2,800.

A search for the term *diluted* reveals that in 2015 Swatch's average number of fully diluted registered shares was 120,069,686, and the average number of fully diluted bearer shares was 30,308,846.[12] That means that the weighted average fully diluted bearer-equivalent share count was 54,322,783. The number 11,344,759 divided by 54,322,783 is 21 percent. So executives and directors together own about a fifth of the company. That's a fair bit.

Compare all this to Fossil. The Texas company's highest paid officer in 2015 was an executive vice president. He made a total of $4,268,722.[13] By American standards, that's unexceptional. What's shocking is what the CEO made. His total compensation for each of the last three years was *zero*.[14]

Fossil's 2015 director compensation was also pleasing. The highest paid member of the board was the lead independent director, who got $234,931.[15]

Regarding ownership, Fossil's directors and officers as a group own just under 14 percent of the company. That's less than Swatch, but still a good amount. But Fossil's proxy statement provides the additional detail that 12.5 percent of the company is owned by the CEO *alone*.[16] It's unclear how much of his personal portfolio this constitutes. But an eighth of a major watch company is no trivial holding.

Consider next related-party transactions. A search for the term *related* in Swatch's annual report turns up the following:

"In 2015, the Hayek Group, owned by the community of heirs of N. G. Hayek, invoiced an amount of CHF 10.2 million to the Swatch Group. . . . This amount primarily covered support for Group Management."[17]

Who's N. G. Hayek? He's the deceased organizer of Swatch Group. Who's in his *community of heirs*? The chairwoman and the CEO are his children, so presumably them. An entity this *community* owns was paid the equivalent of about $10,000,000 during the year. Was this fair? Perhaps that depends on what *support for group management* was.

The report says it was primarily four things: *project management in the construction sector*; *various services relating to the assessment of investment projects, cost control, IT consulting, etc.*; *audit, feasibility studies and process optimization*; and *executive functions*.[18]

*Executive functions.* Are those the same executive functions that the chairwoman and CEO were compensated for directly in their roles as officers of Swatch Group? Hopefully not. What about *the assessment of investment projects* and *cost control*? Aren't those things that management does anyway?

None of this is to suggest malfeasance. But malfeasance needn't be in evidence to justify the rejection of an investment idea. It's not for the investor to find a reason to consider a factor bad. It's for the company to prove that a factor is good.

Fossil also discloses a related-party transaction. In 2015, the son of a director was paid $259,713 in cash and 1,045 in restricted stock units. That's because he was an employee of Fossil's Asia Pacific division.[19] He earned a good salary, but nothing screams impropriety. So Fossil's related-party transaction seems harmless.

Next, look at share repurchases. A search of Swatch's annual report for the term *repurchases* leads to a financial statement note entitled *treasury shares.* This is a common title for a note covering buybacks. *Treasury shares* are shares that are bought back but not *retired.* They can be issued again.

The note says that during 2015 Swatch bought back 77,000 registered shares and 65,000 bearer shares.[20] So it repurchased a total of 80,400 bearer-equivalent shares. That's just the quantity 77,000 divided by five, plus 65,000. In other words, Swatch bought back less than one percent of itself in 2015.

How much did the repurchases cost? To find out, go to the cash flow statement. There's a line called *purchase of treasury shares.* It's a cash outflow from financing. It totaled 28,000,000 Swiss francs in 2015.[21]

A search through the prior year's annual report shows that Swatch bought back stock in earlier years as well. But not much. In 2014 it repurchased 385,000 registered shares and 164,000 bearer shares— a total of 241,000 bearer-equivalent shares—for 107,000,000 Swiss francs. In 2013 it repurchased 17,800 registered shares and no bearer shares—that's 3,560 bearer-equivalent shares—for 2,000,000 Swiss francs.[22] So over the three most recent years the company still bought back less than one percent of itself.

Fossil also bought back stock. Its 10-K details several different *repurchase plans*, and then several distinct *repurchases.* It's the latter that matters. The report first says that in 2015 Fossil bought back 281,000 shares for $28,800,000. The year before, in 2014, it repurchased 4,100,000 shares for $435,000,000. And in 2013 it repurchased 4,900,000 shares for $536,300,000. Additionally, under a newer repurchase plan, the company bought back 2,400,000 shares for $200,700,000.[23] There was a weighted average 48,924,000 fully diluted number of shares in 2015.[24] So all told, over the last three years the company bought almost a fifth of itself.

That's a lot. Was this shareholder friendly? Only if the shares were bought at a discount to worth.

Finally, consider dividends. In 2015 Swatch paid 7.50 Swiss francs per bearer share, and—predictably, per their one-fifth economic interest—1.50 Swiss francs per registered share.[25] Swatch's cash flow statement says that that summed to total dividend payments of 407,000,000 Swiss francs.[26] That's much more than Swatch spent on buybacks.

Fossil, by contrast, paid *no* dividends. In fact, Fossil has *never* paid *any* dividends.[27]

We're not looking at Swatch and Fossil because they both made it unscathed through the value investing model up to this point. To the contrary, both have issues that might have disqualified them earlier. *Market growth assessment*, for example, seems iffy in a world of smartphones. Instead, we're looking at them because they offer interesting contrasts between firms in the same space.

Not every shareholder-friendliness indicator needs to be considered in every case. Often it's best to just look at those factors that jump out. What's *glaring*?

In Swatch's case, what's glaring is the related-party transaction with the executive-owned entity. A $10,000,000 billing is nontrivial. It's not made obvious that this dealing is one that a shareholder would cheer.

Second, executive compensation at Swatch is above average in a Swiss context. This could be ignored *but for the tone set by the related-party transaction*.

The final thing to notice is a positive. It's that management owns a ton of the company.

With Fossil, the main thing that jumps out is repurchases. Over the last three years it spent over a billion dollars to buy a fifth of the company. Some quick math shows that it paid an average of $103 per share. What's coming in the next chapter lets one see if that was a bargain.

Fossil's next glaring factor is executive compensation. It looks good. The highest paid manager is paid appropriately. Better yet, the CEO is a *volunteer*. Plus, he owns an eighth of the company outright. And it's not like he sneaks in some compensation in the form of dividends on his huge stock holdings, because *there are no dividends*.

This lack of dividends is the third thing that jumps out at Fossil. Combined with the buyback program, it suggests a management team convinced that repurchases are the far-and-away best use of free cash flow.

Swatch does not strike me as shareholder friendly. Fossil might, but only if $103 turns out to be well under the company's value per share.

One dicey indicator is enough to compel the astute investor to drop an idea. Shareholder-friendliness is not a four-indicator *average*. It's defined by the *worst*. The fair does nothing to mitigate the danger posed by the foul. Nor should it. After all, gauging shareholder-friendliness is essentially an attempt to answer a basic question: *Do I want to be in business with these people?*

## CHAPTER 14

# Inexpensiveness

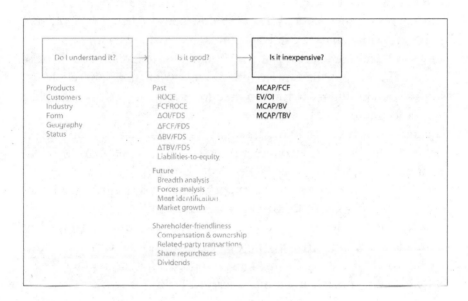

The third step in the value investing model asks a final fundamental question: Is it inexpensive?

Nothing is worth infinity. We can overpay for even the best of companies. So even if we understand a business and find it to be good, we can still make a bad investment by paying too much. Against this specter we deploy *price metrics*. I use four.

First is *times free cash flow*. It equals a company's *market capitalization* divided by its *levered free cash flow*. It's abbreviated MCAP/FCF.

The denominator, levered free cash flow, was covered in Chapter 9. It's *cash flow from operations* minus *capex*. Note that it captures the payment of both interest and taxes.

The numerator, market capitalization, is often shortened to *market cap*. It's the number of shares outstanding times the current price per share.

The market cap of a company is easy to find. It's quoted on financial websites. It can also be figured from scratch. Find the number of shares outstanding in the most recent quarterly report or 10-Q, and multiply that by the current stock price.

Notice the consistency between numerator and denominator. Market cap is the price for the equity *only*. Levered free cash flow is the cash thrown off by the business *after* debtholders have been paid their interest. Hence levered free cash flow goes to the equity holders.

Theoretically, market cap is what it would cost to buy all of a company's outstanding shares. But it's actually an underestimate. That's because the current share price reflects only what *some* shareholders were—moments ago—willing to take for their stock. Most are holding out for more.

Proof of this can be found in acquisitions. Remember LinkedIn? We used it to illustrate accounting principles in Chapter 6. When that chapter was written in the spring of 2016, LinkedIn's stock price was around $135. Then as summer approached Microsoft announced that it was buying LinkedIn for $196 per share.[1]

Why didn't Microsoft just pay $135? Because not all LinkedIn shareholders would part with their stock at that price. Only the most willing would. Coaxing the holdouts required a higher number. They had what economists call a higher *reservation price*.

A second price metric is *enterprise value to operating income*. It's abbreviated *EV/OI*.

The denominator, operating income, was the subject of Chapter 8. It's *revenue*, minus *cost of goods sold*, minus *operating expenses*. Note that it's *not* net of interest or tax expenses.

The numerator, *enterprise value*, is the theoretical takeover price. It's what one would fork over to buy the *entire* company, not just the outstanding shares. Paying it would leave no one else with any financial claim on the company. There'd be no outside common stockholders, no preferred shareholders, no minority partners in subsidiaries, no bondholders, no bank creditors, *no one*.

Enterprise value is a tricky concept, for two reasons. First, it's derived in part from current market prices. So in name, it defies the value investing distinction between price and value. The term *enterprise price* would make more sense.

Second, it's harder to calculate. In essence, it equals *market cap* plus the market price of all of the company's preferred equity, noncontrolling interest, and debt and minus cash.

Like market cap, the enterprise value of a particular company is given on financial websites. Such off-the-shelf figures are convenient. But if a company looks promising, it's wise to calculate enterprise value longhand. To see why, consider its components.

The first component of enterprise value, *market cap*, is already well understood.

The next, *preferred equity*, is simply a different kind of stock. It usually pays a more stable dividend. It's sometimes referred to as *preferred stock* or *preference shares*. If there is any, it's in the equity section of the balance sheet. The amount to add comes from the annual or quarterly report, whichever is most recent.

The next component is *noncontrolling interest*. We saw it in Chapters 6 and 10. Noncontrolling interest is portions of subsidiaries not owned by the company. Sometimes it's called *minority interest*, because it reflects ownership by a minority partner. The number to add is on the balance sheet of the most recent report. It's in the equity section.

This published number for noncontrolling interest is imperfect. It's a carrying value, not necessarily what the minority partner would accept to give up its stake. As such it's an odd fit as part of a theoretical takeover price. Nonetheless, it's usually the best estimate available.

Understanding why noncontrolling interest is added requires a quick dive into investee accounting.

A company can account for an investee in one of three ways. The way that's used depends on how much *control* the company has over the investee. Control is assumed to depend on how much of the investee the company owns. So the accounting method is usually determined by percentage ownership.

This is flawed. Ownership doesn't mean control. Just ask an entrepreneur with a start-up that's 10 percent owned by the leading public company in its industry. What really drives control is the prospect of more funding, access to customers, or a potential buyout. Nonetheless, percentage ownership is what's commonly used.

If the company owns less than 20 percent of the investee, the *cost method* is used. The investment is carried on the balance sheet as an asset at cost, and that's it.

If the company owns between 20 percent and 50 percent of the investee, the *equity method* is used. The investment is initially carried on the balance sheet at cost. When the investee has net income, that net income is multiplied by the percent of the investee that the company owns. This proportionate share of investee net income is then added to the company's income statement. It's called something like *earnings in affiliate*. It flows through to the balance sheet as an addition to the carrying value of the investment.

If the equity method is used, the investee is an *unconsolidated subsidiary* of the company.

If the company owns over half of the investee, the *consolidation method* is used. This makes the investee a *consolidated subsidiary*. The investee's revenue and expenses are consolidated—*mashed in*— with the company's revenue and expenses on the income statement. Further down there's a line called something like *earnings attributable to noncontrolling interest*. That's the amount of the investee's earnings that belong to its other owners. It's the proportionate share of earnings that *aren't* the company's. It's subtracted.

The top part of the income statement dreams that the company owns all of the subsidiary. The lower part wakes it up.

The consolidation method also calls for all of the investee's assets and liabilities to be included on the company's balance sheet. *Noncontrolling interest*—which appears in either the liabilities or equity section, as noted earlier—corrects for the portion of the investee that the company doesn't own.

That is, *earnings attributable to noncontrolling interest* is to the *income statement* what *noncontrolling interest* is to the *balance sheet*.

It's the consolidation method that's most relevant to calculating enterprise value. Noncontrolling interest is added because on the income statement, *earnings attributable to noncontrolling interest* is below *operating earnings*. Operating earnings therefore reflect 100 percent ownership of the investee, which is fiction. But the denominator of EV/OI can't see minority interest. So the numerator has to be fluffed up as if there weren't any.

The last component of enterprise value is debt, both long- and short-term. This could include bank loans, bonds, notes, or any other interest-bearing obligation. The amounts to add are in the liabilities section of the most recent balance sheet.

Calculating enterprise value also requires a decision about cash. Ideally, *excess* cash—that which is obviously not necessary to run the business—is subtracted. It's subtracted because it could theoretically be used to buy out some of the claimants, like bondholders and minority partners. Think of it as *acquisition financing that's already in place*.

But as addressed in Chapter 7, it's hard to know how much cash is truly excess. Financial websites tend to assume that all cash is excess. They automatically subtract it. But that reflects a decision that wasn't expressly made. It can make a company look less expensive than it actually is, creating the risk of overpaying. That's one reason why calculating enterprise value from scratch makes sense.

Another is that there may be more than one line on the balance sheet like *cash and cash equivalents*. For example there could be one called *current financial assets*, or one called *investment securities*. These could include anything from stocks in publicly traded companies to interests in bond funds. Footnotes often clarify their contents.

The more readily these items can be turned into cash at their balance sheet values, the more *cash equivalent* they are. When in doubt, assume that they aren't.

If it's really unclear how much cash is excess, do what we did with *capital employed*. Calculate two versions of enterprise value: one with cash, and one without. Don't buy before both versions put the company squarely in the bargain bin. A good opportunity may slip away, but a potential disaster won't sneak in.

EV/OI is a particularly sage metric. Like *capital employed*, it's blind to type of financing. This contrasts with market cap–based valuation metrics that can be fooled by capital structures.

Consider *market cap to operating income*, or *MCAP/OI*. A company with a lot of debt could look inexpensive just because the numerator prices only the common stock. It doesn't capture the direct cost of buying out any bondholders, noteholders, or bank creditors. But enterprise value is *never* blindsided by capital structure. It prices *everything*.

This highlights a shortcoming of our first price metric, MCAP/FCF. It misses capital structure. So it's dangerous to use by itself. But it's still informative because it offers such a *different* view than does EV/OI. EV/OI weighs the price of the *whole company* against what *accrual* accounting says comes out *before* interest and taxes, while MCAP/FCF weighs the price of the *common stock* against what *cash* accounting says comes out *after* interest and taxes. Using both makes it harder to get bamboozled.

MCAP/FCF and EV/OI both have denominators that come from numbers in the most recent financial statements. But some companies are in industries that are *cyclical*. Demand for their products rises and falls with some exogenous factor. The factor could be the price of a particular commodity, for example.

Cyclical companies often catch the investor's attention because their share prices plunge after a reported drop in income or operating cash flow. These drops can happen because their industry has entered a down cycle.

If the industry is truly cyclical, that down cycle will eventually reverse. Things will boom again. So it can be illuminating to also apply *current* prices to *old* operating results. I call this *backvaluing*. Does the company look inexpensive if today's market cap and enterprise value are weighed against the free cash flow and operating income of last year?

Backvaluing carries dangers. It counts on history repeating. It assumes that the business hasn't fundamentally changed. And it trusts that a historically cyclical industry hasn't actually entered secular decline.

Backvaluing is like a tourniquet. It's a tool that's unsafe to use in all but a narrow set of circumstances.

It's absurd to insist that lousy operating results from a cyclical company in a down cycle are permanent. That's conservatism of an unhelpful sort. So if the industry is *definitively* cyclical, try backvaluing. If there's any doubt, don't.

A third price metric is *price to book*. It equals market cap divided by book value. It's abbreviated MCAP/BV. Book value, recall, equals balance sheet equity.

A final price metric is *price to tangible book value*, or MCAP/TBV. It's MCAP/BV with *intangible assets* removed from the denominator. Patents, trademarks, goodwill, and other assets that aren't physical get subtracted.

MCAP/TBV is a harsher measure than MCAP/BV. It effectively marks any asset that can't be touched down to *zero*. Some situations are better suited to this severity than others. To see which ones, we revisit *goodwill*.

Recall that goodwill equals *acquisition price in excess of book value*. Earlier in Chapter 6, we gave the example of company B having book value of $1,000,000; company A acquiring it for $1,500,000 in cash; and company A increasing the goodwill on its balance sheet by $500,000.

Note the assumption embedded in this practice. Goodwill is an *asset*. So in buying company B and goodwill, company A is swapping assets for assets. That's how accounting sees it. No expense is recognized on the income statement, and no liability is booked on the balance sheet. Nothing *bad* occurs.

What if company A horrendously overpaid? It happens. And when it does, this fact eventually surfaces. Management expresses its disappointment in the wayward new subsidiary and pledges to mop things up. The first swab of the mop is to reduce goodwill by pumping a big part of it through the income statement as an expense. That's a *write-down*: the decrease of an asset on the balance sheet through the recognition of an expense on the income statement.

A fear of write-downs underlies the healthy skepticism that MCAP/TBV offers. It sees goodwill as a write-down waiting to happen. For this reason MCAP/TBV is useful in analyzing companies that have grown by pricey acquisitions.

Both MCAP/BV and MCAP/TBV suffer from distortions caused by repurchases and dividends. But they suffer from them *the same*. What's illuminating, therefore, is the *difference* between the two. If MCAP/BV is reasonable but MCAP/TBV is stratospheric, goodwill is often enormous. This drives the astute investor to assess the wisdom of the company's past acquisitions.

When we calculate price metrics, we get actual numbers. MCAP/FCF may be 5, or 50. EV/OI may be 3, or 30. What's inexpensive, and what isn't?

I like MCAP/FCF to be no higher than 8, and EV/OI to be no higher than 7. Before moving on to benchmarks for the other two price metrics, let's understand what these first two multiples mean.

Imagine that a company's future operating income will be $1,000,000 for each of the next 100 years. Discounting that stream back at—say—10 percent yields $9,999,274. That's from the same spreadsheet NPV function that we used in Chapter 7.

That quantity, $9,999,274, is nearly $10 million. Notice that $10 million is 10 times the forecasted annual operating income.

So if one calculates a company's EV/OI as 10, that could mean that the market thinks operating earnings will be $1,000,000 for each of the next 100 years, and 10 percent is the right discount rate.

Or, it could be mean that the market thinks operating income for the next 100 years will grow 4 percent annually from a $1,000,000 base, and that 14 percent is the right discount rate. Those numbers come from another simple spreadsheet NPV exercise.

In other words, multiples are *shorthand*. They're shorthand for a formal present value analysis. *In them are embedded beliefs about growth rates and discount rates*.

Holding everything else equal, it's better to own a company with income that's growing than one with income that isn't. So when I say that I want EV/OI to be no higher than 7, what I'm saying is that I'll only buy a stream of future operating income *when it's offered to me at a high discount rate*.

Of course one never knows just what future operating earnings will be. Same with free cash flow. And where the exact discount rates come from isn't important. What is important is this: low price multiples signal buying opportunities to the value investor when they reflect *unjustifiably high discount rates*.

The other two price metrics, MCAP/BV and MCAP/TBV, are a little different. They don't reflect a stream of future *anything*. They're multiples of what a company has *now*.

I prefer both MCAP/BV and MCAP/TBV to be no higher than 3. But these are just qualifiers for me. They're not what I *look for*. What I look for is MCAP/FCF and EV/OI. It's worth exploring why.

I aim to own companies that continue as going concerns. I want them *alive*. Profitable ones are worth more that way. But MCAP/BV and MCAP/TBV express price relative to the value of companies *dead*. If a firm stopped operating and sold everything—if it *liquidated*—the total amount available to distribute to shareholders would have something to do with its book value. But when I buy a stock, I don't hope for a stake in some dead company's yard sale. I'm buying a claim on future streams of income and cash flow.

This isn't to say that MCAP/BV and MCAP/TBV are useless. They can uncover opportunities. Say that a company's EV/OI is 9, and that both MCAP/BV and MCAP/TBV are 6. The company doesn't look inexpensive. But MCAP/BV and MCAP/TBV are the same. This leads the astute investor to see if the company owns some juicy tangible asset like land that's carried on the balance sheet at a tiny, decades-old purchase price. Will the company sell the land for cash? Will that cash be excess? If so, all of the price metrics could plunge. That's the kind of useful thinking that the *dead* metrics tease out.

Putting forth my benchmarks so bluntly—8, 7, 3, and 3—is a little dangerous and potentially misleading. It's dangerous because it could be interpreted to mean that it's OK to cut right to valuation without first understanding a business and seeing if it's good. Many investors do that. And it can work. But with that approach mine are not the benchmarks to use.

It's potentially misleading because my benchmarks are actually a little flexible. To see why, think about all the metrics that we've developed so far in this book. Most of them fall into one of three categories.

The first category is *return*. It includes ROCE and FCFROCE. It's concerned with the annual output of a company relative to its committed capital.

The second category is *growth*. It includes ΔOI/FDS, ΔFCF/FDS, ΔBV/FDS, and ΔTBV/FDS. It focuses on how fast something good increased.

The third category is *price*. It's MCAP/FCF, EV/OI, MCAP/BV, and MCAP/TBV. It's about inexpensiveness.

Strength in two of these categories can compensate for averageness in the third. For example, one might be willing to *pay more* for a company that *returned well* and *grew fast*. That is, one might accept a higher EV/OI if ROCE and ΔOI/FDS are high.

By the same token, one might accept an *average* growth rate for a company that *returned well* and is *inexpensive*. For example, a modest ΔOI/FDS might be palatable if ROCE is high and EV/OI is low.

It's tempting to try and reduce the relationship among these three categories to a formula. Theoretically, that could automate investment decision making. But that would distort more than it would clarify, for two reasons.

One, the metrics are *historical*. They're what *happened*, not necessarily what's *happening*. Even the price metrics, which contain current prices, are tied to numbers pulled from old financial statements. We do our best to foresee future operating performance with our four tools of strategic analysis. But that's qualitative. We don't wind up with numbers solid enough to plug into some equation.

Second, the relative importance of each category is different for different investors. This is driven by target holding periods. To long-term investors, return metrics are critical. These shareholders will own companies long enough to see ROCE and FCFROCE govern their actual investment results.

But short-term holders—*flippers*—won't. To them, return metrics are downright quaint. These investors won't own companies long enough to care about anything more than price metrics.

So while it's overreaching to dream up a formula, it's clear that there's some relationship among the three categories. Keeping that in mind encourages slight, constructive benchmark bending.

Note how *late* valuation comes in the value investing model. It follows two time-consuming steps. This contrasts with a more common approach to investment analysis that *starts* with valuation. *What's the earnings multiple?* That's often the first question.

Valuation comes late for two reasons. First, ignorance of valuation fosters objectivity in the earlier steps. It keeps one from being unproductively swayed by apparent cheapness or priciness.

Someone aware that a company looks inexpensive might go easy on it by—for example—underestimating the threat of new entrants. Similarly, someone aware that a company looks expensive might hunt for reasons to reject it, perhaps by prematurely concluding that its supplier base is consolidating.

Of course it's impossible to think in a *total* valuation vacuum. After all, a steep price drop might be why one noticed a company in the first place. But putting valuation last properly focuses one's attention early.

The second reason valuation comes late in the model is because the analyses that precede it are durable. An understanding of a business, and a finding that it's good, both have shelf life. They're valid for a while. They can be called into service whenever a stock price takes a sharp turn.

These sharp turns can come out of nowhere. Remember Kone? In late 2001 Toshiba, the Tokyo-based electronics conglomerate, agreed to buy 4.6 percent of it.[2] Years later in April 2015, Toshiba suffered an accounting scandal. This prompted it to sell some noncore holdings. On July 22, it announced that it had dumped its Kone stake.[3]

Accounting and scandals from Japan would seem unrelated to elevators and escalators from Finland. And yet Kone's stock price dropped 8 percent that week. That's the kind of impact that a sudden share sale can have. And it came out of nowhere. Investors preloaded with an appreciation for Kone were quicker to grasp the situation than those who weren't.

Price metrics often afford us the unsatisfying insight that a company—one that we understand, and one that is good—*isn't* inexpensive. This can be frustrating, since we'd like to buy it. What do we do?

We wait. We wait for years, if necessary. This can be hard to accept. After all, we just expended considerable mental effort to understand a business and to identify it as good. We want a memento of this hard-won conclusion. We want to *do something*.

There are two keys to keeping this restlessness at bay. The first is to recognize the difference between *action* and *progress*. The former readily masquerades as the latter. Action feels productive. It gives a satisfying jolt. But acting for the sake of acting isn't helpful. Accepting this does wonders for one's patience.

A second key is to recognize the *option value of cash*. When we hold cash, we can *do things*. We can buy understandable, good companies at those fleeting moments when they become inexpensive. If we don't hold cash at those times, our options are ugly. We could do nothing, and miss an opportunity. We could sell a different holding, potentially giving up a different upside. Or we could buy *on margin*—with money borrowed from our broker—an unsavory prospect that introduces the upped ante of an interest expense and the specter of a calamitous downside.

Appreciating the option value of cash is hard. It's particularly hard when interest rates are low, when our brokerage statements remind us that we earn almost nothing on reserves. We don't get monthly reports reminding us how clever we are for maintaining flexibility. The option value of cash is never explicitly presented.

That's one reason why the discipline of patience does not come naturally. It's an unintuitive mindset that requires a different perspective. But once we develop it, we make valuation work for us. Our questions get better. *What would the stock price have to sink to such that MCAP/FCF is no more than 8 and EV/OI is no more than 7?* That becomes our limit price. We wait for it.

## Summary

Inexpensiveness can be detected with four different price metrics:

1. Times free cash flow (MCAP/FCF)
2. Enterprise value to operating income (EV/OI)
3. Price to book (MCAP/BV)
4. Price to tangible book value (MCAP/TBV)

Waiting for understandable, good companies to become inexpensive is made easier by recognizing:

1. The difference between action and progress
2. The option value of cash

**CASE STUDY**

## Flowserve Corporation

Flowserve is a major manufacturer of pumps, valves, and seals. Based in Texas, it sells to oil refineries and other industrial facilities. Assume that the business is understandable and good. As of this writing, its share price is $45.50. Is it inexpensive?

Consider first MCAP/FCF. Market cap is $45.50 times the number of shares outstanding. Search for the term *common stock* in the most recent 10-Q:

http://www.goodstockscheap.com/14.1.htm

The seventh hit is note 8, which is titled *earnings per share*. It gives a weighted average common stock figure of 129,781,000. So Flowserve's market cap—the numerator—is $5,905,035,500.

The denominator, free cash flow, is straightforward to calculate. *Cash flow from operations* in 2015 was $417,092,000. That's from the cash flow statement on page 58 of Flowserve's 10-K:

http://www.goodstockscheap.com/14.2.htm

The same page gives *capital expenditures* as $181,861,000 in 2015. How much of that was maintenance? As usual, that's not stated.

Some help can be found in the company's most recent earnings call, for the first quarter of 2016. Right before the 21 minute mark, the chief financial officer says, "We also expect that 2016 capital expenditures will decline compared to the elevated 2015 level when we increased manufacturing capacity in Asia-Pacific and purchased a license enabling increased aftermarket opportunities."

So some of 2015 capex was *definitely* growth. It expanded both manufacturing capacity and *aftermarket*—that is, parts and accessories—opportunities. But how much?

No figure is offered. But note that total capex from each of the two prior years was around $135,000,000. That's about $45,000,000 lower than the 2015 figure. And depreciation—which we know doesn't equal maintenance capex, but that nonetheless is useful for comparisons—was even lower. It was $99,501,000 in 2015. That's from the first third of the cash flow statement.

In the name of conservatism we'll first pretend that the whole $181,861,000 is maintenance capex. Then we'll do a second version that assumes it's $45,000,000 lower, effectively knocking it down to the level of the prior year.

Search the 10-K for *operating leases*, and page 80 reveals that Flowserve has some. Capitalizing them, which would have been done at an earlier stage of the model, means two things for free cash flow. One, it means that lease payments get added back. A search for the term *rental expense* reveals that in 2015 this was $53,100,000.

Two, it means that interest payments on the hypothetical loans used to buy the leased assets get subtracted. This figure can only come from capitalizing the operating leases. So let's tackle that.

Note 10 on page 80 says that Flowserve's scheduled lease expenses are $45,505,000 in 2016, $37,553,000 in 2017, $28,355,000 in 2018, $22,063,000 in 2019, and $18,699,000 in 2020. Enter each year and its corresponding expense into a two-row spreadsheet.

The note then says that starting in 2021 Flowserve has additional future lease commitments of $63,848,000. But it doesn't give the year that the last lease expires. How do we spread this amount out?

Notice how the 2016-2020 lease payments drop somewhere around 15 percent to 20 percent per year. Just roughly continue that trend. Say $15,000,000 in 2021, $12,000,000 in 2022, $10,000,000 in 2023, $8,000,000 in 2024, $6,000,000 in 2025, $5,000,000 in 2026, and $4,000,000 in 2027. That leaves $3,848,000, all of which can go in 2028. One could be more precise, but probably not more accurate. Add all of the 2021 through 2028 figures to the spreadsheet.

Now we need a discount rate. Search for *long-term debt*—the term we successfully used with Gap—and nothing comes up. But the term *senior note* leads to note 10 on page 78. It details three relevant borrowings. The most recent is from 2015, when Flowserve borrowed €500,000,000 at 1.25 percent (a little more, actually, owing to the discount to *par* at which the notes were sold).

Many of Flowserve's operations are in America. But unlike Gap, it also has plenty outside the United States. So Flowserve's borrowing in euros can suggest a discount rate in a way that Gap's borrowing in Japanese yen cannot. That is, Flowserve has leased facilities in Europe that it could buy with euros, but Gap has almost no leased stores in Japan that it could buy with yen. Nonetheless, 1.25 percent strikes me as a little low. I settle on a 2 percent discount rate.

Discounting the 13-year stream of lease expenses at a 2 percent discount rate yields $198,813,374:

http://www.goodstockscheap.com/14.4.xlsx

Multiplying 2 percent by $198,813,374 yields $3,976,267. This is 2015 interest payments.

Free cash flow, the denominator of our first price multiple, can now be calculated. It's cash flow from operations of $417,092,000, minus capex of $181,861,000, plus lease payments of $53,100,000, minus interest payments of $3,976,267. It's $284,354,733. That's the *low* estimate.

The high estimate is $329,354,733. It includes an additional $45,000,000, my crude stab at growth capex.

Dividing these free cash flow estimates by market cap of $5,905,035,500 gives us a range for our first price metric. MCAP/FCF is somewhere between 18 and 21.

The second price metric is EV/OI. The first component of the numerator, market cap, is established at $5,905,035,500.

The next is *preferred equity*. There isn't any, according to the quarterly report's balance sheet. But there is *noncontrolling interest* of $18,321,000. In addition, there are two lines of debt. *Debt due within one year* is $62,566,000, and *long-term debt due after one year* is $1,573,450,000.

On the assets side, cash and cash equivalents is $310,318,000. So the low estimate of enterprise value is $7,249,054,500. That's just market cap, plus noncontrolling interest, plus all debt, and minus cash.

The high estimate assumes that no cash is excess. It's $7,559,372,500.

The denominator, 2015 operating income, is given in the annual report as $525,568,000. But because operating leases were capitalized, two adjustments are necessary. First, lease expense of $53,100,000 must be added back.[4] Then, depreciation is subtracted. Recall that depreciation is assumed to equal the old lease expense minus the new interest expense. Interest was just estimated at $3,976,267. So depreciation is $49,123,733. Therefore, operating income is $529,544,267.

We can now calculate two estimates of EV/OI. Because cash is small, they're about the same. They both round to 14.

The third price metric is MCAP/BV. Book value appears in the 10-Q as *total Flowserve Corporation shareholders' equity*. It's $1,722,665,000. So MCAP/BV is 3.

The last metric, MCAP/TBV, is the same as the prior with the intangible assets removed from the denominator. The quarterly balance sheet shows *goodwill* of $1,240,187,000, and *other intangible assets* of $228,294,000.[5] That makes tangible book value $254,184,000. So MCAP/TBV is 23.

Note that over the last three years Flowserve repurchased about 12 percent of itself. This would have surfaced at the shareholder-friendliness stage of the model. It means that both MCAP/BV and MCAP/TBV are bloated. They're higher than they would be without buybacks.

Nothing here screams inexpensive. MCAP/FCF is 18 at its lowest. That's well above the benchmark 8. EV/OI is 14, double the benchmark 7. MCAP/BV is fine at 3, particularly since buybacks bloated it. But MCAP/TBV is 23, wildly above the benchmark of 3.

The astute investor immediately sees the disparity between MCAP/BV and MCAP/TBV. It's *vast*. It's obviously attributable to goodwill. So even if the stock price plummets, one wouldn't buy before making sure that Flowserve hadn't overpaid for its acquisitions.

Assume for the moment that it hadn't. *What would the stock price have to sink to such that MCAP/FCF is no more than 8 and EV/OI is no more than 7?*

A spreadsheet can easily be put together to answer that question. It allows one to fiddle with the stock price until the price metrics come into line. It shows that Flowserve is inexpensive at $17 a share:

http://www.goodstockscheap.com/14.5.xlsx

But wait. What industry is Flowserve in? Machinery manufacturing. Specifically, the manufacturing of flow control products for the oil and gas businesses.

That's a *cyclical* industry. Demand rises and falls with the price of oil. When prices are down, oil and gas companies constrict their capex budgets. This slows demand for Flowserve's products. But when oil prices rebound, that deferred maintenance roars back as revenue.

Anyone with a car knows that oil prices plummeted in the mid-2010s. In Palo Alto, we went from paying $4 per gallon in the spring of 2014 to paying $2.50 at the end of 2015. Flowserve's 2015 results surely reflect this down cycle. What if Flowserve was *backvalued* to 2014?

The company's 2014 10-K provides the data for this exercise:

http://www.goodstockscheap.com/14.4.htm

Cash flow from operations in 2014 was $570,962,000. Capex was $132,619,000.[6] Some of that was likely for growth, given that depreciation was only $93,307,000. So we'll estimate maintenance capex at $120,000,000.

Assuming the capitalization of operating leases, lease payments of $56,200,000 must then be added back.[7] That's from page 75. And, interest expense should be subtracted. This requires capitalizing the operating leases.

Scheduled future lease expenses are also on page 75: $49,625,000 in 2015, $36,829,000 in 2016, $27,824,000 in 2017, $22,081,000 in 2018, and $17,184,000 in 2019. Then starting in 2020, there's an additional $63,837,000 in lease expense commitments.[8] This can be spread out such that it roughly continues the downtrend. Perhaps $15,000,000 in 2020, $12,000,000 in 2021, $10,000,000 in 2022, $8,000,000 in 2023, $6,000,000 in 2024, $5,000,000 in 2025, and $4,000,000 in 2026. That leaves $3,837,000, all of which gets stuffed into 2027.

As for a discount rate, a search for *senior notes* leads to page 74. It states that the most recent long-term debt financing happened in November 2013. That's pretty timely. It was for $300,000,000, at a rate of 4 percent (actually a little more, again owing to the discount to *par* at which the notes were sold).[9]

Discounting the stream of lease expenses at 4 percent yields $185,506,597:

http://www.goodstockscheap.com/14.6.xlsx

Multiplying 4 percent by $185,506,597 yields $7,420,264. This is 2014 interest payments.

Free cash flow for 2014 therefore equals $499,741,736. That's just cash flow from operations of $570,962,000, minus estimated maintenance capex of $120,000,000, plus lease payments of $56,200,000, minus interest payments of $7,420,264.

Dividing the more current market cap of $5,905,035,500 by 2014 free cash flow of $499,741,736 yields the backvalued MCAP/FCF. It's 12.

On to EV/OI. Published operating income for 2014 is $789,832,000.[10] Because operating leases were capitalized, $56,200,000 in lease expense gets added back, and depreciation gets subtracted. Lease expense minus the just-estimated interest expense of $7,420,264

yields depreciation of \$48,779,736. So 2014 operating income is
\$797,252,264. Backvalued EV/OI is therefore 9 or 10. That's the result
with enterprise value at its estimated low of \$7,249,054,500, and at its
estimated high of \$7,559,372,500.

Not surprisingly, Flowserve looks less expensive when its current
price is held against the operating results of the prior, more successful
year. But that doesn't make it inexpensive. To be truly inexpensive—
provided that Flowserve paid reasonably for its acquisitions, didn't
change markedly between 2014 and 2015, and is in an industry that's
definitively cyclical—the share price would have to drop to \$32:

http://www.goodstockscheap.com/14.7.xlsx

The astute investor—aware that price and worth are different, that
action is not progress, and that cash has option value—waits for a
price no higher than that.

## CHAPTER 15

# Price Drives Risk

It's obvious that buying companies *inexpensively* is preferable to buying them *not inexpensively*. But it's worth exploring why. Doing so shows just how different value investors are from investors of other stripes.

Value investors buy inexpensively for two reasons. First, it increases returns. A future income stream purchased for some amount returns better if the *same* income stream is purchased for a *lesser* amount.

Numbers show the power of this effect. Stock worth $4 that's purchased for $2, and that's eventually priced correctly, returns 100 percent. That is, the quantity 4 minus 2 divided by 2 equals 1.

But if that *same* stock is purchased for $1, it returns 300 percent. The quantity 4 minus 1 divided by 1 equals 3. In this case a halving of price leads to a *tripling* of return.

The second reason is that buying inexpensively *lowers risk*. To see why, consider baseball.

To a runner on first base, the risk of stealing second base is *being tagged out*.

How could the runner reduce the risk of being tagged out? By getting a head start. As the pitcher winds up to throw the next pitch, the runner could creep away from first base toward second. That's allowed. It's called a *leadoff*. It shortens the distance that the runner has to travel to reach the next base.

The runner's conception of risk mirrors that which we put to good use in daily life. Risk is the *chance of a bad outcome*. To lower that risk, we *start closer to the goal*.

What's the risk in investing? *Losing money.* That's what the everyday, practical definition of risk would suggest. And in fact that—or some near variant—is the working definition that most value investors use.

How would the value investor lower that risk? By *investing less money.* Not by buying fewer shares, but rather by buying the *same* number of shares at a *lower price.*

This is well illustrated by an extreme. If a stock were bought at a price of *zero*, there would be *no* risk. There'd be no risk because there'd be no money to lose. It would be as if first and second base were right next to each other.

Chapter 4 noted that a good value investor might expect to beat a standard market index by 500 basis points over time. Chapter 11 then noted that over the last several decades the S&P 500 Total Return was around 10 percent on average. Hence, a good value investor might aspire to an annual average return of 15 percent. That is, 15 percent is the *goal.*

Earlier in this chapter we showed how buying inexpensively increases returns. It brings performance closer to a high standard like 15 percent. So by paying less for a stock, one *starts closer to the goal.*

Value investors see the risk of investing in a stock differently than do most in the money management industry. We define it as the chance of losing money. But the industry defines it as the *average daily change in the price of that stock over the last month.*

The industry calls this *volatility.* It's represented by the the Greek letter sigma ($\sigma$). There are a few math wrinkles to it as well as several variations, none of which we'll cover here. But ultimately, the industry's definition of risk is based entirely on *recent price fluctuations.* There are two problems with this.

First, recent price fluctuations are *historic.* It's what *happened.* They don't necessarily dictate what's *going* to happen.

A stock price isn't like a thrown baseball. The velocity of a thrown baseball is likely to reflect its history. If the ball was descending toward home plate at 80 miles per hour a moment ago, it will probably be descending toward home plate at close to 80 miles per hour a moment from now. That's brought about by *inertia.*

But stocks aren't physical objects. Their movements aren't governed by inertia. As comfortable as it may be to think that they bounce, fly, and ricochet, they don't. They're *stocks*. Expecting them to move like a ball is as silly as expecting a smile from a baseball bat.

The second problem with the volatility view is that it leads to absurdities. Consider two scenarios. In one, a share fluctuated between $2 and $3 over the last month. In the other, that same share fluctuated between $1 and $3 over the same month. The volatility view says that the second scenario is riskier because the price range was wider. It suggests this even if the share was purchased at scenario two's low of $1, which would result in less money at stake than at even the cheapest price offered in scenario one. That's ridiculous.

Ultimately what underlies the volatility view is the efficient market hypothesis. If all investors were rational, the price of a share a moment ago would nicely reflect its worth. So would the price of the share a moment from now.

But think of the *boldness* in that. It counts on people being *so* levelheaded that we can count on their behavior over just the last month—*month!*—to nail down the worth of a stock.

Consider Maui Land & Pineapple, a real estate company in Hawaii. As of this writing, the 30-day high of its common stock was 27 percent above its low.[1] During this period there were no tectonic shifts in company structure, Hawaiian land, or pineapple deliciousness. Do we really think that its *value* fluctuated by 27 percent during the month?

Misguided as it is, the volatility view of risk has strong institutional support. It's easy to see why. Volatility is easier to manage than return, especially in the short term. Over a quarter, it's simpler for a money manager to keep the price range of a diversified portfolio within set boundaries than it is to crank out 15 percent annualized performance.

One can imagine a financial services outfit, troubled by how to deliver above-market rates of return, delighted at the prospect of convincing clients that it's in fact *volatility control* that they want to buy.

Value investing's take on risk upsets another apple cart as well. It's the *risk-return trade-off*. This principle holds that the way to achieve higher potential returns is to take on greater risk. By this logic the road to 15 percent performance is paved with angel investments, misunderstood commodity funds, and emerging market securities of such dubious prominence that not even the United Nations can find the issuing countries.

Value investing doesn't just reject the risk-return trade-off. It *flips it over.* Instead of insisting that outperformance can happen in the face of lower risk, it says that outperformance happens *because* of lower risk.

This perspective gives rise to one of value investing's better-known concepts: the *margin of safety.*[2] It's the big discount that astute investors require to buy shares. It's *the space we allow ourselves to be wrong.* It's why we don't wait for a stock to get a little inexpensive. We wait for it to get *undeniably* inexpensive. Then if we've botched part of our analysis, we're still unlikely to lose significant money. Surprisingly for most, but intuitively for us, covering downsides this way has the happy effect of generating uncommon upsides.

## Summary

1. Volatility and risk are different.
2. The historic price of a stock does not determine the future price of that stock.
3. The volatility view of risk fails to capture purchase price.
4. Buying companies inexpensively both increases return and lowers risk.
5. The volatility view of risk enjoys institutional support, and will continue to do so.
6. Value investing turns the risk-return trade-off on its head.
7. The *margin of safety* is the space that value investors allow themselves to be wrong.

## CHAPTER 16

# Misjudgment and Misaction

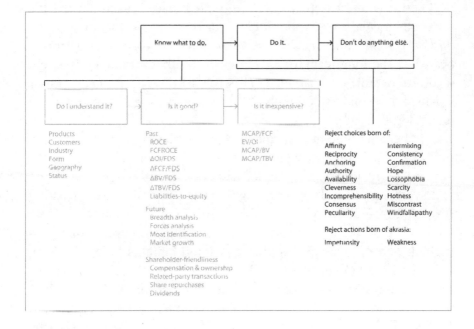

The first three steps of the value investing model—*do I understand it? is it good?* and *is it inexpensive?*—form a row. A lower row, as it turns out, because above it and offset to the right is a row of three supra-steps: *know what to do, do it,* and *don't do anything else.*

The first of these, *know what to do,* is the one that calls for the three lower steps. We *know what to do* after we make sure that we *understand* the business, that it's *good,* and that it's *inexpensive.*

While it's hard for most investors to know what to do, our straight-forward approach makes it possible.

In the Introduction, the value investing model was described as interdisciplinary. It pulls from finance, strategy, and psychology.

*Know what to do* pulls from finance and strategy. But the next two supra-steps—*do it* and *don't do anything else*—are different. They pull entirely from psychology.

To *do it* is to decisively take action when it's time to do so. It means, for example, to buy when an understood, good business is underpriced. This turns out to be *impossible* for most people. It requires one to commit capital to a stock at the precise moment when everyone else seems to be selling it. It demands an on-demand contrarian posture with which most human beings are not endowed.

The third supra-step, *don't do anything else*, is even harder. It's torturous for most everyone. It calls for investing in the value style, *and only in the value style*. Since value is the approach that performs best over the long term, diverting cash to other strategies is likely to dilute overall performance. This means no overpriced glamour stocks, no misunderstood mutual funds, and no angel investments in technology start-ups.

I've personally found this tough. Just try playing soccer with venture capitalists every weekend and keeping your portfolio free of *the next big thing*. I managed, but not without some ribbing.

Psychology went from unrecognized to integral in my investing life. As a freshman economics major at UCLA, I was kept far from the science of the mind. Professors favored the assumption that people behaved rationally, weighing costs and benefits before making choices. Since humans were levelheaded, why dwell on irrationality? Even the physical layout of campus reinforced this split, separating the economics and psychology buildings with a half mile of greenery.

Then in the fall of my junior year—on October 19, 1987—the stock market crashed in what became the largest single-day drop in Dow Jones history. By chance I wore my New York Stock Exchange sweatshirt that morning, which must have looked cheeky, but actually just reflected what had been on top of the clean pile.

Black Monday, as that day came to be known, put the presumption of the sober mind up for review. *How could rational people have made this happen?*

Soon things started to change. Economics departments took a revitalized interest in some earlier studies of investor thinking. *Prospect Theory*, a seminal paper by Daniel Kahneman and Amos Tversky, was passed around. Eventually the efficient market *theory* was downgraded to *hypothesis*. As the years went on, the nascent field of *behavioral economics* grew in prominence to compete with *utility theory* to explain why investors do what they do. By 2015 the American Economic Association had chosen as its president a behavioral economist.

The emergence of psychology didn't shock value investors. They'd been attuned to human whims for decades. In their first book, value investing pioneers Benjamin Graham and David Dodd wrote of "human-nature factors"[1] and "prevailing psychology."[2] In a later book Graham introduced "Mr. Market," a character personifying moodiness.[3] Graham continued to reference psychology in his twilight years of lecturing. Most of these were actually spent at UCLA, where he served as an adjunct professor three decades before I showed up.

By the time I committed to the value approach in 1999, psychology had become accepted as a powerful financial factor. And rightly so. If I had to be stripped of either my psychological awareness or quantitative skills and still make it as an investor, I would without hesitation choose the latter.

I'm no psychologist. But I have seen patterns of irrationality behind people's uneconomic behavior. I've supplemented these observations by studying the works of four experts that I'll credit shortly. That quartet is responsible for any competence I may have developed in the field.

When we identify hazards, we can manage them. So knowing how our instincts can lead us astray is the key to keeping them from doing so. This is why the astute investor rejects judgments born of *cognitive biases*. I focus on 18 of them.

First is *affinity*. Affinity is liking. This bias urges us to buy a stock because we're fond of something associated with it. Perhaps we find the CEO charming, or we're starstruck by the excitement surrounding a new product launch. Of course CEO magnetism and product sizzle are relevant to a company's prospects. But they shouldn't hijack our judgment. They shouldn't be *the reason* that we stick with an idea.

Affinity can also work in reverse. We may prematurely stop considering an investment because we dislike something associated with it. Some long-ago aspect of a company's history may turn us off, as might the abrasive style of a money manager that touts the stock. But these are red herrings. They don't matter.

Second is *reciprocity*. Reciprocity is the tendency to treat others as they have treated us. In finance, it surfaces in institutional settings. Professional money managers are often courted by public company investor relations departments. Gracious treatment gently nudges them toward buying, and away from scrutinizing.

Reciprocity can also work inversely. We may stop considering opportunities that come from sources that we perceive to have done us a disservice. A fund manager not sent an invitation to a company's capital markets day conference, for example, may deprioritize that stock.

Reciprocity is different from affinity. While affinity doesn't require specific action by the investee toward the investor, reciprocity does.

Third is *anchoring*. Anchoring is benchmarking against an insignificant baseline. It can manifest itself as buying just because a price drops from a high level. Anchoring also works on the sell side. An investor may sell an equity just because price soars past its purchase price. What truly matters is price relative to *worth*, not price relative to former price. After all, a stock price that has shot up but that is still below its intrinsic value is likely to increase more.

Fourth is *authority*. The authority bias inclines us toward investment ideas endorsed by those we admire. It's *following*. It's natural for us to seek pointers from people and entities that we respect. But it's wrong to let undue reverence crowd out objectivity.

Correspondingly, the authority bias can motivate us to *ignore* ideas backed by those we consider beneath us. For example, it could cause us to reject an opportunity proposed by someone with less formal education than we have. This is just as unproductive, since good ideas can come from all manner of sources.

Fifth is *availability*. The availability bias emphasizes information that's foremost in our minds, regardless of its overall relevance.[4] Such information may have been obtained recently or presented vividly, or may have reverberated emotionally. For whatever reason, it resonates. We're predisposed to place undue weight on memories that surface with force. This can cause us to overlook other meaningful facts. Investing well requires more balanced recollections.

Sixth is what I call *cleverness*. The cleverness bias inclines us toward ideas that make us feel smart. It favors observations and analyses that require the exercise of mental muscle, ones that afford us the pleasure of swimming in our own intelligence.

Flipped over, the cleverness bias pushes us away from investments that seem too simple. It makes us distrust opportunities that we understand quickly. This is harmful because many worthy investment ideas truly are quite basic.

Seventh is what I call *incomprehensibility*. The incomprehensibility bias causes us to want an investment *more* the *less* well we understand it. It has us conflating *unintelligibility* with *specialness*. It can motivate us to regard the promoter of an obfuscated opportunity as an expert, endowed with a knowledge we couldn't possibly obtain ourselves. Or it can have us hunting for investments described with scholarly jargon, as if circumlocution indicated quality.

Inverted, the incomprehensibility bias causes us to reject opportunities that present plainly. We hate them because they're not hard enough.

The incomprehensibility bias is different from the cleverness bias. The cleverness bias thrives on ideas that are truly complicated, while the incomprehensibility bias just needs ideas to be *expressed* in a complicated way.

Eighth is *consensus*. Consensus is doing what everyone else is doing. It tilts us toward popular investments. This creates the risk of overpaying, since fashionable securities get bid up in price. It's when an investment becomes unpopular—*despised* is even better—that its price can drop to a level that may be below worth.

Of course the *lack* of consensus around an investment idea isn't enough to make it attractive. It might be truly bad. So unpopularity is best thought of as a *necessary but not sufficient* characteristic of a buying opportunity.

Ninth is what I call *peculiarity*. Peculiarity inclines us toward investments that are unique. The opposite of consensus, it afflicts contrarians and those particularly fond of their own ideas. It's similar to the cleverness bias except that it hungers for opportunities that are merely *different*, not necessarily *complicated*.

Acting inversely, the peculiarity bias repels us from ideas that we didn't think of ourselves. It keeps us from learning from others. This limits our universe of opportunities.

Tenth is what I call *intermixing*. It causes us to favor holdings that seem offbeat. It predisposes us to securities that would stand out in our portfolio. To an investor in common stocks, it could make a feature film limited partnership interest look attractive, even though such investments tend to underperform equities.

When the intermixing bias operates inversely, it repels us from opportunities that aren't distinctive. This is like the *peculiarity* bias, but against the background of our *own* portfolio as opposed to that of others.

Note that intermixing is distinct from *diversification*. Diversification is filling a portfolio with different kinds of assets so that not all of them are ever down in price at the same time. It may be an acceptable consideration. But intermixing is picking different assets just for *kicks*.

Eleventh is *consistency*. Also known as *commitment and consistency*, it encourages us to act in concert with our prior actions. It creates an unwillingness to change our mind, particularly when doing so would require us to reverse a position others know us to have taken. It could cause us to buy more of a stock that we already hold, even if real flaws in the issuer have surfaced.

Consistency is different from *perseverance*. Perseverance is sticking with a stock when any contrary indicators that have emerged are inconsequential. In investing, perseverance is a virtue. If a perfectly fine company sees its stock price drop for no good reason, it's wise to hold fast. Consistency, by contrast, is sticking with a stock merely because one already owns it. If the fundamentals of a holding have truly deteriorated, not selling in the name of consistency is a mistake.

Twelfth is *confirmation*. The confirmation bias inclines us toward opportunities that support our preexisting views. It's like *consistency*, but without the need for *actions* as precedent. Mere *beliefs* suffice.

Correspondingly, the confirmation bias repels us from ideas that run counter to our convictions. It causes us to reject good opportunities because they fall outside of our conception of a trend, an industry, or a market. It creates the risk that we'll prematurely stop looking at worthwhile opportunities. In addition, it robs us of the chance to update our beliefs to better reflect reality.

Thirteenth is *hope*. As much a disposition as a bias, hope urges us to *believe* in an investment. It has us curating available information to make the positive stand out. Correspondingly, it has us suppressing any unflattering data

In many spheres of human life hope is a virtue. In sports, it can drive us to run faster, bike farther, or jump higher. In entrepreneurship, it can help us to sell convincingly, or to lead effectively. But in most listed company investing, there's no opportunity for hope to manifest itself in a useful way. Stocks don't welcome our optimism. They don't *care* if we believe in them.

The fourteenth is what I call *lossophobia*. It's more formally known as the *fear of loss*. It's the panic that sires irrational stabs at capital preservation. We feel it when we have the urge to place a sell order as the price of a holding drops, even though the fundamentals of the company remain solid. If the fundamentals have truly deteriorated, selling may be appropriate. But equating a price drop with a worth drop never is.

Lossophobia might be thought of as a type of *pessimism*, that is, the *hope* bias operating inversely. It's such a durable part of investor psychology that brokerages created a product to serve it: the *stop-loss order*. This innovation triggers an automatic sale when the price of a holding dips below a certain price. It not only fails to use a dip as an opportunity to buy, it *guarantees a loss*. A better name for it would be a *make*-loss order.

Fifteenth is *scarcity*. The scarcity bias predisposes us toward investments that we perceive to be in short supply. The rarer it seems, the more we want it. Promoters of initial public offerings leverage this bias when they tout an IPO as *oversubscribed*.

Correspondingly, the scarcity bias repels us from opportunities that seem abundant. It can make deals that are easy to access look bad, as if availability itself indicated low quality.

Scarcity also works on the sell side. If we own stock in a deteriorating company whose price has yet to fall, we may delay selling since the chance to do so at an acceptable price seems lasting.

The sixteenth is what I call *hotness*. It's the belief that one is on a *roll*. More formally called the *hot hand fallacy*,[5] it surfaces after a string of good investment outcomes. It wells up as the sense of being on a *winning streak*. The next buy, the feeling goes, will benefit from the same magic that graced the last.

Operating inversely, hotness causes us to withhold investment after a few consecutive bad results. We may come to believe that we're on a *losing streak*.

The seventeenth is what I call *miscontrast*. This bias causes us to favor investments that aren't good in an absolute sense, but merely better than others we're seeing at a particular time. It's founded on the fallacy that a low caliber of current opportunities will sustain. It creates the risk that we'll tie up capital in a marginal investment, leaving us without the money necessary to participate in a truly great one when it surfaces. It strips us of the option value of cash. Miscontrast often surfaces during times when stock prices are so high that bargains are scarce.

The eighteenth is what I call *windfallapathy*. It's an admittedly makeshift portmanteau meaning *apathy caused by a windfall*.

People who receive a lot of cash unexpectedly—a big inheritance, for example, or proceeds from the sale of a family business—may develop a certain carelessness toward investing. They may commit capital to frothy IPOs, or to chancy emerging market securities. It can almost seem as if they're trying to whittle their net worths back down to prior levels.

Windfallapathy is understandable. Dropping one's investment standards may serve as a reminder that money isn't as scarce as it once was. It may also provide the temporarily pleasant sensation of feeling *big*. But bad investing leads to real losses, erasing any newfound financial peace. However playful it looks at onset, windfallapathy is a bias best neutered early.

The mere *presence* of a potential source of misjudgment does not by itself make an opportunity bad. It's only bad when a cognitive bias *dominates* choice, overriding objectivity. For example, seeing what admired investors do is a reasonable way to generate investment ideas. It's not necessarily the authority bias in action. It only is if the model doesn't recommend the investment *and one makes it anyway*.

That's why the judgments to reject are those *born of* cognitive biases. To be born of something is to *exist just because of it*.

Several cognitive biases can act simultaneously. For example, if a respected investment bank pushes an IPO that's oversubscribed, both the authority and scarcity biases can be conjured. This can strengthen their detrimental impact. It certainly has in my case.

In the preface, I outlined three investment mistakes that I made. Each was born of several cognitive biases teaming up to dupe me.

In the first, I failed to sell my Coca-Cola Company shares even though their price had clearly flown past their worth. Why? *Affinity* played a part, as I liked the company's iconic status. *Authority* was also involved, since a respected money manager held on to her Coke stock. In addition *consistency* was complicit, since holding was a way for me to confirm my earlier praise of the company's enduring value.

What about by premature sale of Nike? *Anchoring* drove me, since I compared the company's soaring stock price to the small amount that I had paid for it. So did *authority*, as a famous investor had just sold his Nike stock. *Consensus* acted similarly, since most funds I followed either didn't own the stock or were selling it.

My failure to buy Mueller Industries also came from a cocktail of misjudgments. The *intermixing* bias acted inversely, since Mueller would for me have been just another industrial equity in a portfolio containing several. *Miscontrast* also operated inversely, as Mueller was one of several good options I was considering at the time. Finally *peculiarity* may have been at work, since the company was suggested to me by a peer.

I'm happy to report that all of these errors happened years ago. But I'm aware of my susceptibility and remain vigilant for another.

Note that the 18 cognitive biases give a sort of *credit* to the investor. We can empathize with someone who, for example, is under the sway of the consensus bias. The investor's bad decision can be *explained away* by the influence of others making the same poor choice. Through the perverse lens of consensus, the misjudgment made sense.

But what if there is no misjudgment, but there is a *misaction*?

I've seen this. During the 2008 financial crisis, several acquaintances of mine sold listed stock fund interests at deep losses. These were intelligent people. They knew about cognitive biases, had no pressing needs for cash, and were justifiably confident that higher prices would eventually return. One of them had even been a student of a recognized pioneer in behavioral economics. Yet they all sold. It was as if they *failed on purpose*. Why?

This phenomenon of *acting against one's better judgment* is not new. Neither is humankind's quest to explain it. It was well addressed by Aristotle, the ancient Greek philosopher. He called it *akrasia*, meaning *lack of restraint.*

In his *Nicomachean Ethics*, Aristotle defined two sorts of akrasia. Each is a pitfall that can joyride investor conduct even in the absence of misjudgment.

The first sort of akrasia is *impetuosity.* It's acting on an urge. It's doing something without thinking about it. It's hard to fight, because it feels like the instincts that serve us so well in sports, personal relationships, and other spheres of life.

Beating back impetuosity hinges on recognizing it as *fleeting.* It feels strong when it wells up, but it subsides just as sharply. But choices made under its influence last. They can result in permanent losses of capital, a result that's anything but fleeting.

The second sort of akrasia is *weakness.* It's passively capitulating to passion *after deliberation.* It's doing something fully aware that it's foolish.[6] This was the sort of akrasia that my acquaintances gave in to during the financial crisis.

Weakness can seem indistinct from the source of misjudgment that it masks. Picture a panicked shareholder selling stock in an excellent company when the price plunges for no good reason. Was it *lossophobia* that forced the sale? Or was the shareholder aware that selling was wrong, and just succumbing to *weakness*? Clearly, there's some overlap. But this inelegance carries the benefit of redundancy. It provides multiple lenses through which to spot errors in the making.

Akrasia is troubling. It's human nature at its most feeble. Understanding its genesis is hard. But it's quite real. People partake of all manner of indulgences—consciously and unconsciously—that do them harm. When akrasia sets its sights on investors, it causes economic damage that sustains.

Aristotle is one of the four thinkers that I referenced earlier, one that I rely on to better understand how we all think. I embrace his views on akrasia fully.

The other thinkers are contemporary. One is Robert Cialdini, an American psychology professor. Cialdini studied sales situations. He found that good sales professionals use some combination of six methods to inspire customers to buy: affinity, authority, commitment and consistency, consensus, reciprocity, and scarcity. Value investors were quick to repurpose his findings. They saw the six methods as reasons why financial actions that shouldn't be taken *are* taken.

Cialdini's book *Influence* is a masterstroke of insights. It's an accessible distillation of his academic research. Investors who have read it enjoy an unparalleled advantage. A finer unwitting contributor to the practice of value investing can hardly be imagined.

The last two experts are the psychologists Daniel Kahneman and Amos Tversky. Among much else, these two collaborators brought the availability bias to light.

It's easier for misjudgment and misaction to hurt a shareholder today than it was when I started investing in 1989. Back then, news that sparked an investor to act often came from a physical newspaper. To trade required putting down the newspaper, picking up the telephone, calling a stockbroker, and placing an order. That lumbering operation contained breaks during which haste could be arrested. The lulls in that bygone process gave reason a chance to prevail.

The Internet has erased those circuit breakers. Today, it's typical for an investor to scan financial news in one browser window and trade with an online broker in another. With smartphones, one needn't even sit down. The pauseless flow denies prudence the opportunity to intercept goofs in the making. So baking reflection into the investment process is more helpful now than ever.

Once one accepts psychology as a force, it can be harnessed to advantage. I try to put it to work for me. Before placing a buy or sell order, I tick through the list of 20. I consider the 18 cognitive biases and the two forms of akrasia. I ask, is this the authority bias acting? Is this the reciprocity bias acting? And so forth. The process doesn't take long, and it occasions just enough introspection to keep me from doing something foolish. I may still make a mistake, but it's less likely to be of the psychological sort.

Just knowing the dangers of an activity does a great deal to inoculate us against them. That's why we give the sources of misjudgment and misaction simple labels. It helps us to catch them early. When we feel them welling up within us we can pause, regain our mental footing, and act in ways that will bear fruit for years.

## Summary

Investor misjudgment is caused by some combination of 18 cognitive biases:

1. Affinity
2. Reciprocity
3. Anchoring
4. Authority
5. Availability
6. Cleverness
7. Incomprehensibility
8. Consensus
9. Peculiarity
10. Intermixing
11. Consistency
12. Confirmation
13. Hope
14. Lossophobia
15. Scarcity
16. Hotness
17. Miscontrast
18. Windfallapathy

Investor misaction is caused by one of two forms of akrasia:

1. Impetuosity
2. Weakness

# PART III

# MAINTENANCE

# CHAPTER 17

# Portfolios and Selling

When an understood, good company gets inexpensive, we buy its stock. But how much?

My rule is simple. Provided that I have enough uninvested cash, I put 10 percent of the portfolio in it. I've seen other good investors use infinitely more complicated guidelines, but none that I've found to be more practical.

If I'm not comfortable putting at least a tenth of the portfolio into an equity, I don't want the equity. If my conviction is lower I don't buy less, I buy *none*.

A strong conviction is important in part because right after a buy the price of a stock is almost certain to *drop*. That's the corollary to another near-certainty: that the price paid for a stock is unlikely to be a low. Rock-bottoms don't send out invitations. So knowing when one will happen is impossible. The astute investor counts on missing them.

Correspondingly, I prefer not to put *more* than a tenth of the portfolio into a single equity. This reduces the chance that I'll lack the cash necessary to take advantage of other opportunities that emerge.

Buying is one aspect of portfolio construction. Another is selling.

There are two problems with selling. The first is taxes. As noted in Chapter 4, the profitable sale of stock is taxable in most circumstances. Just how much this eats into long-term returns is best illustrated by example.

Picture two portfolios. Each starts with only cash, buys only non-dividend-paying stocks, and liquidates after 30 years. Assume that any stock sales are subject to a total long-term capital gains tax rate of 30 percent.

Portfolio one uses all its cash to buy stock on the first day. It appreciates 15 percent before taxes every year. It doesn't sell anything until the liquidation date, at which point it immediately pays any taxes due.

Portfolio two also uses all its cash to buy stock on the first day. It too appreciates 15 percent per year before taxes. But it churns its holdings *annually*. At the end of every year, it sells everything, and uses all the after-tax proceeds to instantly buy different stocks. When it liquidates after 30 years, it too promptly pays any taxes due.

Portfolio one would end the 30-year period with more money. But what's striking is just how much more. It would wind up with over *twice* as much cash. That's because every year when portfolio two paid its capital gains taxes, it whittled down the amount set to grow at 15 percent over the following year. In other words, *ongoing tax payments stunted the power of compounding*.

By contrast, portfolio one's capital was *never* whittled down. It regularly got to multiply its 15 percent by a bigger number:

http://www.goodstockscheap.com/17.1.xlsx

Of course one could never count on an equity portfolio to appreciate at exactly 15 percent annually, and the chance of immediately finding stocks to replace just-sold ones is low. Plus the 30-year period is arbitrary, and a 30 percent tax rate doesn't apply to everyone. But however simplified, this example highlights the toll that frequent selling takes.

The second problem with selling is alternatives. Companies that are understood and good don't go on sale every day. They're hard to find. So absent an acute cash requirement, each stock sale mandates a hunt for the next opportunity.

Even with these problems, selling does makes sense in some instances. I see four. The first is when price flies past value. If EV/OI is over 25, and there are no mitigating facts, I find it hard to justify holding.

The second instance is when a company that originally registered as good turns out not to be. This could be because the original analysis was wrong. Perhaps the threat of new entrants was stronger than it first appeared, or a market thought to be growing really wasn't. Or it could be because circumstances have changed. Maybe a once-mighty retail chain has come under pressure from online-only sellers, or a company that thrived under regulation has faltered in deregulation.

The cognitive bias of consistency can make it hard to see such instances. We may want to hold just to validate our buys. But analyses really can be wrong, and contexts really can change. Selling in such situations keeps a snag from ripping into both a realized loss and a missed chance to redeploy cash into a better opportunity.

The third instance is when one is bought out. Public companies sometimes get acquired. As we saw in Chapter 14, such transactions often happen at a premium to the recent trading price. A vote may be put to shareholders on the matter, but for everyone other than major stakeholders, it's perfunctory. One effectively has no say.

I've been bought out several times. I dislike it. It turns a pleasantly appreciating investment into a taxable event. But if profitable, given the absence of practical options, it makes sense to accept such sales.

The fourth instance is when cash is needed to make an investment that's clearly better than one already held. The problem with this is that fresh ideas often glow with a special promise. They're *new*. The hope bias gets a prime shot at causing mischief. As such, I get extremely suspicious of my reasoning when I think that I'm spotting such a circumstance. I've never actually sold one company for the specific purpose of buying another.

Two commonly cited reasons for selling puzzle me. One is *rebalancing*. It's selling part of a stock holding because appreciation has caused it to represent a disproportionately large percentage of the portfolio.

Rebalancing makes sense to those who equate risk with total portfolio volatility. I don't. So on the sell side, I've never seen the merits of this practice. It makes more sense to me on the buy side, since unless part of a holding was sold, a decrease in its portfolio prominence means that its price dropped. One could now buy more of it *cheaper*. But on the sell side rebalancing looks to me like the anchoring bias in action.

A second common reason for selling is to prove that an investment was a success. The sale is seen as a sort of finish line. Underlying this perception is a view that cash is somehow *more real* than stocks.

It's not. Cash and stocks are different forms that wealth can take. Unrealized gains are not endemically less concrete than realized gains. Selling doesn't demonstrate investing competence any better than does intelligent holding.

There's an additional reason that selling happens. It relates only to institutional portfolios, like hedge funds. It's about compensation.

Chapter 1 noted that investment funds often pay managers 2 percent of assets under management per year, plus 20 percent of any gain above some hurdle. That 20 percent is applied to *pre*tax returns. It's blind to taxes. For this reason professionals may emerge as more enthusiastic about selling than would their limited partners. After all, unless they're tax-exempt, the limited partners are the ones that come to bear the bulk of the tax liabilities born of the fund's realized gains.

One faces great impetus to sell. It feels good. It's conclusive. It turns the brokerage statement into a congratulations card. But it also triggers a tax expense and—short of a pressing need for cash—forces a search for the next underpriced equity. When a sale is wise, its justification is distinct. It's an overpricing, an analytical error, a contextual change, a buyout, or a better opportunity. Absent that clarity, I hold.

Even without active selling, an equity portfolio can generate cash. It can do so in two ways. The first is through acquisitions, as mentioned earlier.

The second is through dividends. Dividends can become sizable. This fact gets lost in the commonly quoted metric of *dividend yield*.

Recall that dividend yield equals annual dividends divided by current stock price. But to an owner, *current* only counts in the *numerator*.

When I first bought Nike stock, the dividend yield was around 2 percent. Over a decade later when I sold it, it was still around 2 percent. But by then *my* dividend yield—the current annual dividend divided by the price *I'd* paid for the stock—was closer to 10 percent. Dividends had gone up over time, but my cost hadn't. That's how dividends can become a booming cash source underappreciated by all but those who get them.

Remember that my portfolio is *concentrated*. It contains no more than a dozen names, and usually far fewer. On purpose, it's not diversified. Many good equity portfolios are, but mine isn't.

I choose to concentrate because I've observed over time that good, focused stock portfolios outperform diversified stock portfolios. This is because diversified portfolios are more like an index. They have more names in them. The more a portfolio *looks* like an index, the more it *behaves* like an index. It's hard to both resemble and outperform something.

Of course a *bad* focused equity portfolio can certainly lag a diversified stock portfolio. Concentration isn't *enough* to assure outperformance. But if it's purposefully constructed, a focused group of inexpensively bought good companies is particularly promising.

While I don't diversify *within* my equity portfolio, I do diversify *outside* of it. I always keep enough cash on hand to cover expenses for a few years. As I get older, I expect to increase this number of years.

This isn't cash inside the equity portfolio waiting to be invested in stocks. It's cash *outside* of the equity portfolio, held in federally insured banks. It will never be anything other than *cash* or *spent*.

Sequestering cash enables me to confidently ride the wild price swings guaranteed to come with a concentrated equity portfolio. It's what lets me take the long view. When the price of my stock portfolio halved during the 2008 financial crisis, I didn't panic. I knew that I could meet all of my expenses. There was no *basis* for panic.

Many governments insure bank deposits. Coverage varies by country. In America, the Federal Deposit Insurance Corporation generally guarantees up to $250,000. In the United Kingdom, the Financial Services Compensation Scheme stands behind £75,000. In Canada, the Canada Deposit Insurance Corporation backs C$100,000.

Because the whole point of sequestered cash is to avoid the scare that forces ill-timed stock sales, it's wise to stay well under the insured limit. Opening up accounts at several different banks is not hard.

Sequestered cash is best held in the same currency as one's expenses. If it isn't, foreign exchange rate fluctuations can hurt one's ability to meet obligations.

As I write this, the British pound has slumped to a 30-year low against the U.S. dollar. This follows Britain's decision to leave the European Union.[1] Some American investors think the slump is overdone and have invested in the British pound.

To people whose expenses are in U.S. dollars, those pounds don't count as sequestered cash. Instead, they count as a *currency investment*.

Two things that may look like good repositories for sequestered cash really aren't. The first is *certificates of deposit*, or *CDs*. Outside of the United States they're commonly called *time deposits*. They offer higher interest rates than do regular bank accounts. Money must stay in them for a predetermined period. If it's withdrawn early, a penalty is applied that more than wipes out the extra interest.

If the CD interest rate is *much* higher than the regular interest rate, one could theoretically keep a portion of sequestered cash in CDs. The portion would have to be limited to that which shouldn't be needed for the duration of the lockup period.

That said, I don't use CDs. Since the timing of cash needs can surprise, I prefer to keep the focus of sequestered cash on costless accessibility.

The other repository is cash-like funds. They too offer higher interest rates. An example is a fund that invests in *commercial paper*. Commercial paper is short-term notes issued by corporations.

Such cash-like vehicles usually behave like cash. One can pay bills with them. But I've seen instances when they don't. During the financial crisis, an acquaintance of mine was surprised to learn that her financial institution had temporarily halted withdrawals from such a fund. She couldn't make payments with it.

This potential—the inability to immediately liquidate—is the problem with these alternatives. The purpose of sequestered cash is to free one from worry during equity market gyrations. If what's used for expenses ever *can't* be used for expenses, that benefit is lost. One can wind up having to sell part of an equity portfolio when it's underpriced, erasing the benefits of stock investing.

Cash has its own problems, of course. Inflation erodes its purchasing power over time. Expansionary monetary policies—*governments printing money*—exacerbate this. But if held in government-insured accounts under applicable limits, at least it's always there. That availability is what makes the interim ups and downs of an equity portfolio's price not only bearable, but almost trivial.

## Summary

1. Conviction prepares one for the likely price drop that follows a stock buy.
2. Selling stocks can make sense when price flies past value, when a company thought to be good turns out not to be, in buyouts, or when a clearly better opportunity emerges.
3. The problems with selling are taxes and alternatives.
4. Questionable reasons for selling include rebalancing, memorializing success, and industry compensation.
5. Equity portfolios can generate cash without active selling through buyouts and dividends.
6. Good focused equity portfolios outperform diversified equity portfolios over the long term.
7. Cash sequestered for ordinary expenses in government-insured accounts makes equity portfolio price gyrations less troubling.

# CHAPTER 18

# Endurance

What if a company being considered for investment turns out to do something that one thinks is morally wrong?

Not illegal. Not against any regulations. But *wrong*. Something about its customers, its tactics, or its leadership strikes one as ethically off.

Maybe the company uses a dominant market position to beat family-owned businesses into insolvency. Perhaps its management team is insufficiently diverse from a gender or an ethnic perspective. Or possibly it's the very nature of its products, because they're unhealthful, addictive, or dangerous.

Whatever it is, something in one's makeup—upbringing, religion, or just a conviction on how civilization should work—shoots a sharp message: *the world would be better off without this firm.*

I don't raise this issue as some sort of moralist. I'm not a philosopher, missionary, or member of the clergy. I raise it for practical reasons.

To achieve long-term after-tax outperformance, one must hold on to stock in good companies for a long time. It's easier to do this with a portfolio that's consistent with one's moral posture. Not exemplary or praiseworthy, just *consistent*. Otherwise, a sudden awakening of principles could compel one to sell stocks for an uneconomic reason. If that happens when prices are down, financial health suffers.

It's therefore useful to define one's ethical disposition early. I've seen smart people do it in one of four ways.

The first is *amorality*. It's not viewing investing through an ethical lens. It regards money management as an activity that sits outside of moral consideration. Put differently, it sees the ethical imperative of investing as growing wealth.

The second is what I call *moral failure abstention*. It's *not* investing in companies with certain unsavory characteristics. It's a list of *don'ts*. It often entails dismissing firms that make certain products. Cigarettes and handguns are two common current examples.

The third is what I call *moral success affirmation*. It involves investing *only* in companies with certain desirable characteristics. It's a list of *do's*. Again, this is commonly related to a firm's products. A popular current example is renewable energy.

Fourth is what I call *moral failure activism*. It involves *buying* stock in companies with *undesirable* characteristics for the purpose of pushing for change as a shareholder. It's premised on stockholders having more influence over company affairs than do mere citizens. For example, shareholders may be able to force a *shareholder proposal* onto the agenda of a company's annual general meeting.

My purpose in sketching out these four ethical postures is not to advocate one over the other three. My purpose is to encourage the picking of one—or of some variant—to avoid a hiccup in performance later on.

Practicality may not be the only good reason to define one's moral posture. But it's the one that's easiest to accept. And while one's ethical views can change over time, I've observed that they tend to change less than other facets of an investor's makeup. It's an enduring feature with which the investor reckons, either early and painlessly or later and less so.

## Summary

There are four different moral postures toward investing:

1. Amorality
2. Moral failure abstention
3. Moral success affirmation
4. Moral failure activism

# CHAPTER 19

# Generating Ideas

The value investing model needs to be fed stock ideas. These ideas can come from different sources, some of which are more fruitful than others. I look at seven.

The first source is bad news. Stories about companies often emphasize an extreme element of an event. These extremes get amplified in headlines. Headlines drive human reaction, sometimes too far. This can cause stock price swings deeper than would a more sober take on the facts.

Overreactions don't just come from individual investors. They come from professional money managers as well. For example, a hedge fund doesn't want to scare off its limited partners when it reports holdings at the end of a quarter. As such it may dump a perfectly good company going through some passing embarrassment.

Sometimes a news-driven stock price drop may be warranted, but overdone. Take Anheuser-Busch, the maker of Budweiser beer. In 2005, newspaper articles appeared suggesting that beer's days were over.[1] Alternatives like vodka with Red Bull were gaining ground with younger drinkers. I analyzed Anheuser-Busch and found it to still have a thriving core business. But the stock price dropped anyway.

As I was turning this over, dad invited me to the baseball game in San Francisco. I can't remember who the visiting team was, or who won. But I do remember what I saw: *people drinking a lot of beer.*

My observation hardly qualified as advanced market research. Plus it happened in an American ballpark, a natural context for beer drinking. But it was real. Beer's days weren't over. Shortly afterward I paid $45 per share for stock in Anheuser-Busch.

Three and a half years later, in November 2008, the company was acquired for $70 per share. Including dividends, that investment delivered an average annual return of around 15 percent. I neither sought nor liked the buyout, as Chapter 17 would suggest. But taxes on gains are the preferred kind of financial pain.

Other times a news-driven stock price drop is fully justified. For example, Volkswagen's share price plunged following an emissions scandal that emerged in September 2015.[2] While the situation is still playing out as of this writing, it appears that there was in fact an organized effort within the company to skirt regulations. That's bad. Plus, Volkswagen didn't register as good before the crisis. Its ROCE was underwhelming. To the astute investor hoping to hold for decades, the situation presented little opportunity.

On rare occasions a news-driven stock price change is totally unjustified. This can happen because a story affecting one company leads to trading in the stock of another. For example, online messaging company Twitter chose TWTR as its stock ticker symbol in preparation for its November 2013 IPO. This caused a wild surge-and-crash cycle in TWTRQ, the common stock of bankrupt electronics retailer Tweeter Home Entertainment Group.[3]

Bad news can involve real tragedies. Security breaches compromise privacy, train crashes cause injury, and foodborne bacteria spark illness. No investor of conscience wishes for these mishaps.

But sensationalist reporting can trigger dislocations that don't make sense. The gap between price and value yawns. The astute investor is meant to bridge it. Good investing has no friend like bad journalism.

A second source of ideas is *spin-offs*. A spin-off is the public listing of a company that was previously part of another listed company.

The spin-off process generally starts with a distribution of shares in the newly independent entity to the old parent's shareholders in the form of a dividend. Then those new shares start trading.

Often, some of the old parent's shareholders are institutional investors. When their spin-off shares start trading, they may sell them automatically. This is because the new stock doesn't meet their formal investment criteria, such as a minimum market cap. This forced selling can depress the price of shares in companies that, if they're both understood and good, are worth owning.

A third source is regulatory filings. Many governments require large investors to periodically report their holdings. These filings are public. One can compare reports between periods to see which stocks talented professionals bought.

In America, money managers with at least $100 million in assets under management are required to file a quarterly report that lists—with some exceptions—their U.S. stock holdings. Called a *13F*, the report is due 45 days after the close of a quarter. They're posted at www.sec.gov. Check midway through February, May, August, and November.

Mining 13Fs has many limitations. Understanding them helps to make the tactic work.

The first limitation is that one has to know which professionals are worth following. Outperforming mutual fund managers are easy to spot, since their track records are public and clear. But private fund managers may share their records only with clients. And professionals that run portfolios inside larger companies—even listed ones—may never detail their histories.

One can't really know if a professional is worth following before seeing a track record. Fame is not a proxy for performance. I am routinely struck by the high profile of some perennial laggards, and the anonymity of some total stars.

A second limitation is that 13Fs disclose only long positions. They don't disclose short positions. This makes them useless for studying managers that pair long and short positions in what are effectively single bets. It's potentially dangerous to mistake the visible long half of such a bet as the full bet.

Third, 13Fs don't disclose the prices paid for shares. One can research the low for a quarter and safely conclude that the price paid was not below that. But greater specificity isn't available.

A fourth limitation is the time lag. In the 45 days since the end of the quarter, stocks just bought could already have been sold. Correspondingly, positions sold could have been reestablished.

Fifth, the filing itself can drive the price of a stock up. When a well-known professional buys something, many blindly follow. This can end any inexpensiveness that once helped to make the stock attractive.

Sixth, a stock appearing for the first time on a 13F may not have actually been bought. It may have been received in a spin-off. A money manager may even have started selling it between the date of receipt and the date of the filing. It could be the *opposite* of an idea worth considering.

Seventh, the authority bias can push one to play copycat. A psychologically undisciplined investor can unthinkingly mimic a master. But masters make mistakes. It's better to view the debut of a stock on a 13F as an invitation to analyze from scratch.

A different cognitive bias can push one away from reading 13Fs. It's the peculiarity bias. It can make 13F mining seem parroty. Dirty, even. But that's misguided. Consider an analogy.

Imagine a restaurateur with a downtown restaurant. Every quarter, the restaurateur receives in the mail a letter from a trusted authority. The letter discloses the major actions taken by the most successful restaurant in the country. One quarter it might say that the exemplary establishment raised soft drink prices by 5 percent. The next quarter, it bought a new fryer. And so forth.

Would the restaurateur throw out the letter without reading it? Of course not. It's informative and accurate, and might contain a useful idea. It's like the best trade magazine imaginable, free and errorless. Plus the restaurateur accepts no obligation to do whatever the better establishment did just by reading.

An investor ignoring 13Fs is like the restaurateur throwing out the letter. It's an odd, limiting act. A better approach is to read select 13Fs fully aware of their shortcomings, secure in the knowledge that autonomy is not sacrificed. One isn't required to replicate a hero's trade any more than the restaurateur is required to buy a new fryer. A disclosure is not a directive.

The fourth idea source is *reorganizations*. Often shortened to *reorg*, a reorganization is a transformative event in a company. It could be a merger, a big change in capital structure, or the sale of a major division. It often involves complications that only an investor comfortable with complexity would care to sort out.

Such complications repel many. This limits the universe of potential buyers. A lower share price can result.

A fifth source is *small capitalization stocks*. Also called *small-caps*, these issues generally have market caps under $2 billion.

Companies this size can be hard for institutional investors to buy, for two reasons. For one, they may be prohibited by charter from buying stocks with a market cap below some threshold. Second, even if they're allowed to buy small-caps, it might not be useful for them to do so.

Picture a $50 billion mutual fund that sees promise in a $500 million market cap firm. Even if it buys 10 percent of the company, and that stake doubles in price, the needle on the fund's overall performance would barely budge. The gain would be just one-tenth of one percent of the fund. So the investment wouldn't be worth making.

These two factors leave many small-cap stocks untouched by a big part of the asset management universe. The result can be lower share prices worth pursuing for those running smaller amounts of capital.

Small-cap investing can take on some of the characteristics of *activism*. Activism is agitating for change in owned companies. It can come with small-cap investing for two reasons. First, sometimes it's necessary. Small-cap company management teams may take advantage of the absence of big institutional investors to do things that they wouldn't with greater oversight. Second, it's possible. Small-cap executives may be more accessible than large company executives. Presidents quickly returning e-mails is not unusual. In short, small-cap investing can occasion a deeper involvement with holdings, something that the astute investor readies for.

A sixth source is *stock screeners*. Stock screeners are Internet tools that filter stocks according to quantitative parameters. They're often based on valuation metrics. One might fetch a list of stocks ranked by their price to book ratio, for example.

Stock screeners aren't my favorite source. To the long-term holder interested in first understanding a business and seeing if it's good, starting with valuation is putting the cart before the horse. Additionally, stock screeners can call attention to companies in outlying financial situations that wouldn't interest someone looking to hold for life. Nonetheless, many strong investors get good at tapping this source for ideas.

Seventh is *serendipity*. Serendipity is the mental preparedness to receive tips from everyday life. It requires being engaged with the world. While driven by chance, it doesn't strike randomly. It favors the open mind.

I first became interested in the Swedish company Clas Ohlson when I noticed that every time I went into one of their Stockholm hardware stores, there seemed to be *a lot of customers buying a lot of things*. I analyzed the company and found it to be good. Had I not been receptive to ideas that crop up unexpectedly, I might not have noticed it.

Incidentally, this particular find didn't play out perfectly. The stock never got inexpensive enough for me to buy. Plus, I got a little overzealous in my search for disconfirming evidence.

During travels around Sweden, I would pop into stores just to make sure that the chain's appeal wasn't limited to Stockholm. It wasn't. They all had customers. Then late one afternoon at the end of a weekend in the city of Helsingborg, I walked into the Clas Ohlson store on the main pedestrian mall. Empty. *Gotcha, Clas Ohlson.* As I was peeking down the aisles to make sure that I hadn't missed anyone, a woman called over from behind a counter, "Pardon, but we're closed."

Serendipity is also useful in reaching conclusions about companies already under consideration. In 2012 I was analyzing Tesco, the British grocer. Investors I admired owned it. Also, I'd recently been floored by its express store on Monck Street in London. It had everything that I'd come for, all located right where I expected.

Serendipity intervened the next month, back in California. I noticed an ad for a new chain of supermarkets called Fresh & Easy. It turned out to be owned by Tesco. I visited the store closest to my house, in the city of Mountain View. Product quality was high, prices were fair, and the staff was attentive.

Of course the staff was attentive—*I was the only customer.* I stopped my analysis. Since then Tesco's stock price has plunged, due in part to a drop in same-store sales to which my neighborhood Fresh & Easy clearly contributed. It's closed now.

Serendipity is great with consumer-facing industries like retail. They're exposed. But one may be familiar with other, less universally visible industries because of a job or background. It works there, too.

Serendipity has the pleasant effect of boosting the relevance of ordinary environments. Everything is evidence. The logos on people's shoes, the number of passengers on the plane, the brand on the broken escalator—all can inform judgments about what people buy, what companies make, and what products work. This doesn't condemn one to a life at a heightened state of alert. Rather, it offers a spigot of ideas whose handle the astute investor controls.

The seven sources are mere inspirations for the model. None of them credential an idea to pass through with preferential treatment. In fact, once one feeds an idea into the model, it's best to forget where it came from.

The advantages of this practice are clear. When we forget that we're looking at a company because it's a spin-off, it's owned by a hero, or its stock price plunged, we keep a whole raft of cognitive biases at bay. We get raw material worth processing, plus the clear mind needed to process it well.

## Summary

Promising sources of investment ideas include:

1. Bad news
2. Spin-offs
3. Regulatory filings
4. Reorganizations
5. Small-caps
6. Stock screeners
7. Serendipity

## CHAPTER 20

# Differences Among Value Investors

The distinction between price and value is the sole requisite principle of value investing. It's the only *must*. Beyond that, there are valid differences in approach. I see eight.

First is *asset class*. Listed equities return best over time, as addressed. But there are practitioners able to squeeze performance out of other sorts of holdings. Bonds work for some, real estate works for others. They're tougher rows to hoe, but some hoe them well.

A second valid difference is *holding period.* Some value investors plan to hold what they buy for just months. Others hope to hold indefinitely. Different timelines occasion different priorities.

For example, short-term holders consider *catalysts*. A catalyst is a reason that a price could soar from the depressed level that helped to make a security attractive. Unexpectedly good quarterly results could be a catalyst, as could the dismissal of an unpopular executive.

Catalysts are less interesting to long-term investors. They're too near-term a concern. Never intending to sell, I don't give them a thought.

A third valid difference is *activism*. As noted in the prior chapter, activist investors agitate for change in the companies that they own. They might be viewed as *their own catalysts*.

The alternative is staying uninvolved. It's the choice of most investors, both good and bad. I call it *inactivism*, since *passive* implies index fund investing.

Activism requires an extraordinary level of gravitas and tenacity. People who are feared and skilled in this specialty are the ones that achieve the best results. Activism is not something in which one fruitfully dabbles.

Fourth is *diversification*. Some value investors have diversified portfolios, with perhaps 50 or more names. Others prefer *concentration*, with fewer than 10.

These thresholds depend somewhat on the amount of money managed. A $50,000 portfolio spread out among a dozen different stocks might be considered diversified, while a $10 billion fund invested in a dozen names might seem concentrated.

Diversification tends to decrease volatility, should that be a goal. But as Chapter 17 noted, the more diversified a portfolio is, the harder it is to beat a relevant index.

One way to appreciate this is through the *law of large numbers*. It's a principle from probability. It says that the more times an experiment is run, the closer the average result will be to the expected result. In investing, the expected result is the index's return. So the more names in the portfolio—each name being an experiment, in the parlance of the law—the closer the portfolio's return will be to that of the index.

Some stripes of value investing force one into a diversified portfolio. Small-cap investing can, since there aren't that many shares traded of each company. They're *small*. So a small-cap investor that adds $100,000 to assets under management might have to find a new name because the ones already owned don't have enough shares available to buy.

A fifth valid difference is *quality*. Our approach has been to focus on how good a business is in an absolute sense, before considering price. We labor over historic performance metrics, strategic positioning, and shareholder-friendliness. We look for quality.

But an equally convinced group focuses on buying companies that are inexpensive relative to how good they are. To them garbage is fine, as long as it's cheap garbage. Some in this group get exceptional results.

My focus on company quality reflects three of my other preferences: inactivism, concentration, and a long holding period. What I buy has to be good because I'm not going to fix it, I've only got a few others like it, and it's mine forever.

These preferences aren't about great foresight or morality. They're about taxes. Unrealized appreciation isn't taxed in the United States, so everything else being equal, holding is advantageous. I draw a straight line from tax policy to investment policy.

Sixth is *leverage*. Leverage is debt. What is true for operating companies is true for investors: debt amplifies results. When an investor buys on margin, results that would otherwise be good become exceptional, and results that would otherwise be bad become catastrophic. The potential of the latter keeps many value investors away from debt. But not all.

Seventh is *complexity*. Some value investors prefer simple setups. They like common stock in straightforward companies. I do, as the model makes clear. But others like it complicated. They may seek convertible bonds that become equity only under hard-to-forecast circumstances. They may prefer stock in development-stage pharmaceutical companies undergoing clinical trials, or in technology companies whose fortunes are dependent on the outcome of pioneering research.

They adore these complications not because they're falling prey to the cleverness bias. They adore them because it gives them less buy-side competition. Other investors will simply abstain from trying to sort out convoluted situations. This can keep prices lower than they would be otherwise.

Eighth is *shorting*. Shorting is a way to bet on a stock price's decline. It involves selling stock without actually owning it, by renting it from someone who does, with the goal of profiting when the price falls.

Shorting is theoretically attractive. It promises a way to benefit from a finding that a security is overpriced. But it's thorny to implement. Shares to rent can be hard to find, fees can be high, and a *short squeeze* can cause a price meant to plunge to actually soar.

Despite these complications, some value investors do short. But many do so as agents, not as principals. That's because it increases their compensation. Shorting is a hallmark of a complicated fund. As noted in the first chapter, it's the kind of stunt that managers attempt in order to justify compensation schemes of 2 percent plus 20 percent. It's a ticket out of the land of 1 percent.

Of the eight dimensions on which value investors can differ, two invite suspicion. Shorting is one. It just doesn't work that well. I know of no principals that both rely on shorting and outperform over the long term.

Leverage is the other. While debt can be milked for bonus returns much of the time, one big margin call can be enough to foul years of solid results.

I nonetheless include shorting and leverage on the list to allow for the possibility that they could be made to work under some circumstances. But they're dicey. They're back doors out of the kingdom of value investing and into a land of some other, less practical strategy. Some would say that this invalidates them as intelligent tactics. To those with long-term perspectives, something that doesn't work sometimes can ultimately be indistinguishable from something that doesn't work at all.

## Summary

Dimensions on which bona fide value investors can differ include:

1. Asset class
2. Holding period
3. Activism
4. Diversification
5. Quality
6. Leverage
7. Complexity
8. Shorting

# CHAPTER 21

# Preservation

Losing money is worse than not losing money. That's obvious. But behind this truth lies some math that's worth sketching out. It makes clear why value investors act conservatively.

Picture a portfolio that realizes a 50 percent loss in a year. Not one that started the year with stock that just happens to have halved in price 12 months later. One that actually *realized* a 50 percent loss. One that began on January 1 with cash, bought stock during the year, sold that stock later in the year, and on December 31 had half as much cash as it started with. What would it take for the portfolio to get a fresh start?

It would need a 100 percent return the next year just to get back to zero. That's *hard*. Recall that with my Anheuser-Busch 15 percent return I was *elated*.

This is different from other activities. Consider soccer. If a player takes a shot on goal and misses, nothing happens to the score. The player gets a fresh start with the next ball. But if soccer was investing, the player would get negative points for missing. Goals would be required just to get back to zero.

That's why value investors behave with such restraint. We put capital preservation first. We do so because the mathematics of our missed shots is punitive.

When capital preservation is underemphasized, returns suffer. Returns suffer because losses add up like weights. This truth isn't evident to those who believe in the risk-return trade-off. They see the subordination of capital preservation as a step *toward* outperformance. And those believers constitute the *majority*.

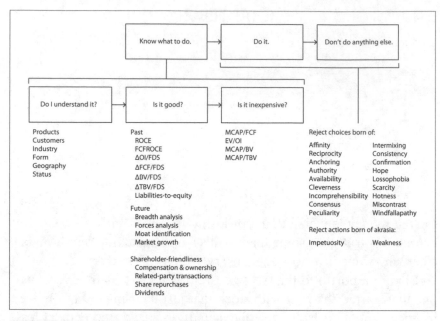

**FIGURE 21.1: The value investing model**

Perhaps that's why the asset management industry has such staggering failure rates. Most actively managed equity funds—those that pick individual stocks—don't beat basic market indexes.[1] *Most*. That's the output of a blind majority.

Two practices help to preserve the value investing model's ability to repel losses.

The first is to keep it current. Think of the model as having three layers (Figure 21.1). The top layer is the general guidance: know what to do, do it, and don't do anything else. The middle layer gets more specific, insisting that investments be understood, good, and inexpensive. The bottom layer is more specific still. It's all of the lower text: the six parameters of understanding, the historic operating metrics, the cognitive biases, and so forth.

The top layer is permanent. Knowing what to do, doing it, and not doing anything else is so durably commonsensical that one might even apply it to other endeavors.

But the bottom layer could change. Both accounting standards and disclosure requirements will evolve. For example, the Federal Accounting Standards Board might mandate some new calculation of operating income such that ROCE has to adapt. Or perhaps the SEC will eliminate related-party transaction reporting such that the number of shareholder-friendliness indicators has to be trimmed down to three. The more time that has passed since the publication of this book, the more important it is to be aware of such developments.

The second practice is to think in percents. One should focus on the total return expressed as a percentage, not on currency amounts. A 20 percent realized loss is not okay just because the actual damage was only $1,000. And a $1,000,000 gain is not impressive if it represents just a 2 percent annualized return.

Thinking in percents nurtures habits that perform faithfully over a lifetime. Discipline learned in the early years of little capital works just as well in the later years of more capital. New tricks aren't required just because of more zeroes.

When one thinks in percents, the absolute gains follow. They follow because value investing is remunerative. That provides most practitioners with enough motivation to stay with the strategy. But since I committed to it at the end of the last century, I've come to see that value investing has other benefits as well.

For one, it keeps me engaged with the world. Turn on the serendipity spigot, and suddenly everything applies. Shopping, news, traffic—all become inputs just as worth processing as financial statements. The instants and fragments of everyday life become relevant in a vivid way.

Second, value investing is, at root, truth seeking. It takes inherently hazy situations and chases the facts. *What's this thing worth?* I see a realness in that.

Third, it rewards a long-term perspective. It compels me to consider how enterprises will develop over time. Part of that drill is picturing civilization years forward. That carries an aspect of foresight that I like.

That long-term perspective applies on a personal level as well. I hope to keep value investing long after other lines of work would have become difficult. Making presentations, attending meetings, and flying overseas all get harder with age. But value investing requires none of that. I'll do it for as long as I have all my marbles. My younger loved ones are standing by to let me know when the first one plinks out.

Above subsistence and below gluttony, there's little correlation between net worth and happiness. Money just doesn't produce life's great joys. Those come from those loved ones, from health, and from other sources that don't care much about geometric means, depreciation schedules, or enterprise values.

But an absence of money can keep one from the great joys. And therein lies value investing's promise. It gives one the freedom to fully embrace what really matters. To be able to drop everything and lavish attention on such gifts, fearlessly, and at times of one's choosing—

That, I think, is what rich is.

## Summary

1. Capital preservation is a value investing priority because of the mathematics of realized losses.
2. The risk-return trade-off blinds most asset managers to the primacy of capital preservation.
3. Most actively managed equity funds fail to beat basic market indexes over time.
4. The bottom layer of the value investing model is the part most likely to change.
5. Thinking in percents encourages habits that work over a lifetime.
6. Value investing has benefits beyond remunerativeness.

# GLOSSARY

*Terms introduced in this book appear with an asterisk.*

**Absolute**
A basis for assessing investment returns that involves comparisons to a fixed percentage.

**Account payable**
An amount owed to a vendor. An item in the *liabilities* section of the *balance sheet*.

**Accrual basis**
An accounting presentation based on rules of *revenue* and expense recognition, as opposed to *inflows* and *outflows*.

**Accrued expenses**
Periodic amounts owed but not yet paid, like salaries. An item in the *liabilities* section of the *balance sheet*.

**Activism**
An investment approach that involves agitating for change in a company as a shareholder.

**Affinity bias**
A cognitive tendency that preferences one toward things one likes for peripheral reasons.

**Akrasia**
The cognitive dynamic that encourages acting against one's better judgment.

**Amorality**
An ethical posture that sees investing as exempt from moral consideration.

### Amortization

The decreasing of the *book value* of an intangible, *noncurrent asset* by recognizing periodic expenses on the *income statement*.

### Anchoring bias

A cognitive tendency that urges *benchmarking* against insignificant baselines.

### Arithmetic mean

The sum of a set of numbers divided by the number of numbers in the set.

### Asset class

A group of securities with similar characteristics whose prices tend to move together in response to certain events.

### Assets

Things that a business controls, finds valuable, and bought. A *balance sheet* section. Separately, a synonym for *investments* or *holdings*.

### Audited

Examined by a public accountancy, as with a *listed* company's annual report.

### Authority bias

A cognitive tendency that encourages one to follow leaders unthinkingly.

### Authorized shares

The number of shares of *stock* that a company is allowed to issue according to its charter or bylaws.

### Availability bias

A cognitive tendency that urges decisions based on information easily recalled. Introduced as the *availability heuristic* in the 1973 paper *Availability: A Heuristic for Judging Frequency and Probability*.

### Backvaluing*

A method of valuing *issuers* in cyclical industries whereby current security prices are weighed against prior period operating results.

### Backward integration

A business's expansion into an activity performed by a supplier.

### Balance sheet

A *financial statement* that measures a business at a single point in time by subtracting *assets* from *liabilities* to yield *equity*.

## Basis point

One one-hundredth of one percent.

## Bearer share

*Stock* that conveys ownership rights to whoever holds the stock certificate.

## Benchmark

A quantitative standard.

## Bonds

Securities that represent a promise to pay back a borrowed amount plus interest.

## Book value

Purchase price less *depreciation* of a *noncurrent asset*. Separately, a synonym for *equity, shareholders' equity, owners' equity,* and *net assets*.

## Breadth analysis*

A test of the robustness of a company's groups of customers and suppliers.

## Capital appreciation

Increase in market price.

## Capital employed

A measure of a company's required financial base. Generally calculated as *total assets* minus *excess cash* minus *non-interest-bearing current liabilities,* and possibly minus *goodwill*.

## Capital expenditure

The purchase of an *asset* of material cost that will last for more than one year. A *cash flow statement* item. Also called *capex* or *purchase of property, plant, and equipment*.

## Capital lease

A lease reflected on the *balance sheet*. Also called a *finance lease*.

## Capital structure

The totality of a company's financing, particularly as it relates to the proportion of debt to *equity*.

## Capitalized

Recognized as a *noncurrent asset* on the *balance sheet*.

## Cash basis

An accounting presentation based on *inflows* and *outflows*.

## Cash flow from financing

The section of the *cash flow statement* concerned with borrowings and the sale and repurchase of an *issuer's* own securities, like *stock*. Also called *cash flow from financing activities*.

## Cash flow from investments

The section of the *cash flow statement* concerned with the purchase and sale of *assets* of material cost that will last for more than one year. Also called *cash flow from investing activities*.

## Cash flow from operations

The section of the *cash flow statement* concerned with a company's core activities. Also called *operating cash flow* or *cash flow from operating activities*.

## Cash flow statement

A *cash basis* financial statement that describes a business over a period of time.

## Catalyst

A reason that a *stock* price could move, particularly in the near term.

## Circle of competence

The range of businesses that one is capable of understanding. Introduced in Berkshire Hathaway's 1996 annual report.

## Cleverness bias*

A cognitive tendency that preferences one toward ideas that require a high level of intelligence to understand.

## Commercial paper

Short-term debt securities issued by corporations.

## Concentration

The practice of allocating capital among a limited number of *assets* or *asset classes*. The opposite of *diversification*.

## Confirmation bias

A cognitive tendency that preferences one toward ideas that support pre-existing views.

## Consensus bias

A cognitive tendency that preferences one toward popular things.

## Consistency bias

A cognitive tendency that preferences one toward actions that are in concert with prior actions. Introduced as *commitment and consistency* in the 1984 book *Influence*.

## Consolidated subsidiary

An investee that an *issuer* accounts for using the *consolidation method*.

## Consolidation method

A way an *issuer* accounts for an investee that is generally over 50 percent owned.

## Cost method

A way an *issuer* accounts for an investee that is generally less than 20 percent owned.

## Cost of goods sold

Expenses that a business incurred specifically in producing *revenue* during a period. An *income statement* item. Also called *cost of revenue*.

## Current assets

*Assets* that could be used within a year. A *balance sheet* subsection.

## Current liabilities

Obligations that must be settled in one year or less. A *balance sheet* item.

## Debt to equity ratio

A measure of the manageability of a company's debt load. Calculated as financial debt divided by *equity*.

## Deferred income

Advance payments received by a company for products not yet delivered to customers. An item in the *liabilities* section of the *balance sheet*.

## Depreciation

Decreasing the *book value* of a tangible, *noncurrent asset* by recognizing periodic expenses on the *income statement*.

## Direct method

A way of preparing the *cash flow from operations* section of the *cash flow statement* that begins with *inflows*.

## Diversification

The practice of allocating capital among different *assets* or *asset classes* for the purpose of avoiding overexposure to any single variable. The opposite of *concentration*.

## Dividend

A payment made by an *issuer* to its shareholders, generally in cash, and generally quarterly or annually.

## Dividend yield

Current annual *dividend* divided by current *stock* price.

## Earnings before interest and taxes

*Operating income* plus *non-operating income*. An *income statement* item. Also called *EBIT*.

## Earnings before taxes

*Earnings before interest and taxes* minus interest expense.

## Efficient market hypothesis

A proposition from economics that holds that the price of something equals its worth.

## Empiricist

One who derives knowledge from experience, not theory.

## Enterprise value

The theoretical takeover price of a company. Generally calculated as *market capitalization* plus the market price of *preferred equity*, *non-controlling interest*, and debt; and minus cash.

## Equity

A *balance sheet* section that equals *assets* minus *liabilities*. Also called *shareholders' equity*, *owners' equity*, *net assets,* or *book value*. Separately, a synonym for *stocks* or *shares*.

## Equity method

A way an *issuer* accounts for an investee that is generally between 20 percent and 50 percent owned.

## Excess cash

Cash on a company's *balance sheet* that is not necessary to maintain current operations.

## Financial statement

A quantitative description of a business, such as an *income statement*, *cash flow statement*, or *balance sheet*.

## Fixed income

A type of security that promises to pay set amounts, like a *bond*.

## Form 10-K

An annual report filed with the Securities and Exchange Commission by American companies.

## Form 10-Q

A quarterly report filed with the Securities and Exchange Commission by American companies.

## Form 13F

A quarterly report filed with the Securities and Exchange Commission by American money managers with at least $100 million in *assets* under management that lists certain holdings, generally American *equities*.

## Form 20-F

An annual report filed with the Securities and Exchange Commission by non-American companies that issue *stock* on American stock exchanges.

## Forward integration

A business's expansion into an activity performed by a customer.

## Free cash flow

The amount of cash that a company produces by operating. Broadly calculated as *cash flow from operations* minus *capital expenditures*.

## Free cash flow return on capital employed

A *cash basis* measure of the profitability of a business that equals *free cash flow* divided by *capital employed*. Also called *FCFROCE*.

## Fully diluted shares

*Shares outstanding* plus the number of shares that could become outstanding upon exercise or conversion of other securities, such as options.

## Fundamental analysis

A method of evaluating *stocks* that focuses on individual *issuers* as opposed to macroeconomics or general trends.

## Geometric mean

A type of average better suited to growth rates than *arithmetic mean*. Also called the *compound annual growth rate*.

## Goodwill

Acquisition price in excess of the *equity* of the acquired entity. An intangible *asset* on the acquirer's *balance sheet*.

## Growth capital expenditures

*Capital expenditures* made to expand a business. Also called *growth capex*.

## Hope bias*

A cognitive tendency to believe that optimism can positively influence an outcome.

## Hotness bias*

A cognitive tendency to believe that good outcomes will be followed by a good outcome. Introduced as the *hot hand fallacy* in the 1985 paper *The Hot Hand in Basketball: On the Misperception of Random Sequences*.

## Impetuosity

*Akrasia* in the form of giving in to an urge.

## Inactivism*

A common investment approach that involves buying securities with no intention of influencing the *issuer*. The opposite of *activism*.

## Income

*Revenue* minus expenses. An *income statement* item of which there are several variants. Also called *earnings*.

## Income statement

An *accrual basis financial statement* that describes a business over a period of time. Also called a *consolidated statement of operations*, a *profit and loss statement*, or a *P&L*.

## Incomprehensibility bias*

A cognitive tendency that preferences one toward obfuscated propositions.

## Indirect method

A way of preparing the *cash flow from operations* section of the *cash flow statement* that begins with *net income*.

## Inflow

Cash entering a business.

## Ingrainedness*

A source of *moat* born of prominence in a distribution channel.

## Initial public offering

The first instance of the sale of securities on a *public* exchange. Also called an *IPO*.

### Interest coverage ratio

A measure of the manageability of a company's debt load. Generally calculated as *earnings before interest and taxes* divided by interest expense.

### Intermixing bias*

A cognitive tendency that preferences one toward investments that stand out from those already in a portfolio.

### Intrinsic value

Worth as determined by *fundamental analysis*, not market price.

### Inventory

A *current asset* poised to become a *cost of goods sold*. Also called *stock-in-trade*.

### Invested capital

A measure of a company's required financial base. Generally calculated as the sum of capital committed by shareholders, debtholders, and any other parties expecting a financial return.

### Issuer

An entity that offers for sale its own securities, such as *stock*.

### Law of large numbers

A principle from probability that says that the more times an experiment is run, the closer the average result will be to the expected result.

### Leverage

Debt, or the prominence of debt in a *capital structure*. Also called *gearing*.

### Levered free cash flow

A measure of *free cash flow* that captures interest payments.

### Liabilities

Obligations, calculated as *assets* minus *equity*. A *balance sheet* section.

### Liabilities to equity ratio

A measure of the manageability of a company's obligations. Generally calculated as total *liabilities* divided by *equity*.

### Listed

Traded on an exchange. Also called *public*.

### Long

The state of owning outright, as with *stock*. The opposite of *short*.

**Lossophobia bias***

A cognitive tendency that urges incurring minor losses as a way to avoid greater losses. Formally known as *fear of loss.*

**Maintenance capital expenditures**

*Capital expenditures* made to replace *assets* wearing out. Also called *maintenance capex.*

**Margin of safety**

The outsized discount to worth that *value investors* demand before buying a security. First appeared with this meaning in the 1934 book *Security Analysis.*

**Market capitalization**

*Shares outstanding* times current share price. Also called *market cap.*

**Miscontrast bias***

A cognitive tendency that preferences one toward currently available bad things just because they're better than currently available worse things.

**Moat**

A figurative barrier that protects a business from competition.

**Moral failure abstention***

An ethical posture that discourages investing in companies with certain unsavory characteristics.

**Moral failure activism***

An ethical posture that encourages buying stock in companies with unsavory characteristics for the purpose of agitating for change as a shareholder.

**Moral success affirmation***

An ethical posture that encourages investing in companies with certain righteous characteristics.

**Negative cash cycle**

An atypical situation where a company gets paid by customers before it pays vendors.

**Net income**

The bottommost measure of *income* on the *income statement.* Calculated as *revenue* minus all expenses, including interest and tax. Also called *profit*, *net profit*, or the *bottom line.*

### Noncontrolling interest

Portions of *subsidiaries* not owned by the *issuer*. Also called *minority interest*.

### Noncurrent assets

*Assets* that take more than a year to use. A *balance sheet* subsection. Also called *long-term assets*.

### Noncurrent liabilities

Obligations set to be settled in more than one year. A *balance sheet* subsection.

### Non-operating income

Earnings from peripheral activities. An *income statement* item.

### Normal cash cycle

The typical situation where a company pays vendors before it gets paid by customers.

### Operating expenses

Expenses recognized by a business regardless of what was sold during a period. An *income statement* item. Also called *selling, general and administrative expenses*, or *SG&A*.

### Operating income

*Revenue* minus *cost of goods sold* and *operating expenses*. Also called *operating earnings* and *operating profit*. An *income statement* item.

### Operating lease

A lease that is not reflected on the *balance sheet*.

### Outflow

Cash exiting a business.

### Peculiarity bias*

A cognitive tendency that preferences one toward unique investments.

### Preferred equity

A kind of *stock* that's senior to common stock, and that generally pays a relatively stable *dividend*. An item in the *equity* section of the *balance sheet*. Also called *preferred stock* or *preference shares*.

### Present value

A stream of future cash flows discounted back at some rate such that it can be expressed as a single amount in current terms.

### Price to book

A price metric generally calculated as *market capitalization* divided by *equity*.

### Price to tangible book value

A price metric equal to *price to book* with intangible *assets* removed from the denominator.

### Proxy statement

An annual filing with the Securities and Exchange Commission made by American companies that includes information on compensation and related-party transactions. Also called a *DEF 14A*.

### Real estate investment trust

A type of American real estate entity that distributes at least 90 percent of its taxable *income* to shareholders in the form of *dividends*. Also called a *REIT*.

### Realized

Actualized through a sale.

### Rebalancing

The common asset management industry practice of maintaining target allocations among *assets* or *asset classes* in a portfolio through periodic buying and selling.

### Reciprocity bias

A cognitive tendency premised on treating others as they have treated us.

### Registered share

*Stock* that conveys ownership rights to its registered owner.

### Relative

A basis for assessing investment returns that involves *benchmarking* to an index.

### Reorganization

An *issuer*'s merger, recapitalization, or other transformative event. Also called a *reorg*.

### Repurchase

A company buying back its own shares. Also called a *buyback*.

### Retained earnings

*Net income* not paid out as *dividends*. An *equity* item on the balance sheet.

### Return on capital employed

A measure of the profitability of a business. Generally calculated as *operating income* divided by *capital employed*. Also called *ROCE*.

### Revenue

The sum of sales during a period reported on an *income statement*. Also called *turnover*.

### Risk

The chance of a bad outcome.

### Risk-return trade-off

A principle from finance that holds that higher potential returns are achieved by accepting greater *risk*.

### Scarcity bias

A cognitive tendency that preferences one toward things that appear to be in short supply.

### Secondary offering

A *public* offering of securities that have already been *listed*.

### Selection bias

An information distortion whereby a data set's characteristics are incorrectly represented by a cherry-picked portion of that data set.

### Shares outstanding

The number of shares of *stock* in a company held by shareholders. Also called *basic shares*.

### Short

The state of having sold a security that was rented, rather than owned, in an effort to profit from a price decline.

### Small capitalization stocks

Shares in companies with a small *market capitalization*, generally under $2 billion. Also called *small-caps*.

### Speculating

Making an investment in the hope that it can be sold at a higher price, without *fundamental analysis*.

### Spin-off

The *public* listing of a company that was previously part of another *listed* company.

**Stock screeners**

Internet search tools that filter *stocks* according to quantitative parameters.

**Stocks**

Ownership stakes in corporations. Also called *shares* or *equity*.

**Straight line basis**

A method of *depreciation* whereby the same amount is expensed each period.

**Strike price**

The price that must be paid to convert an option, warrant, or other security into *equity*. Also called *exercise price*.

**Subsidiary**

An entity over which an *issuer* exercises a degree of control.

**Switching cost**

An expense of money, time, or other resource triggered by a change, generally of a supplier.

**Times free cash flow**

A price metric generally calculated as *market capitalization* divided by *levered free cash flow*.

**Total return**

A measure of investment performance that includes *dividends*.

**Treasury shares**

*Stock* bought back but not retired. An item in the *equity* section of the *balance sheet*.

**Unconsolidated subsidiary**

An investee that an *issuer* accounts for using the *equity method*.

**Understanding statement***

A clear sentence that defines a business's products, customers, industry, form, geography, and status.

**Unlevered free cash flow**

A measure of *free cash flow* that does not capture interest payments.

**Unrealized**

Not actualized through a sale.

### Value chain

A set of sequential commercial activities, either in an industry or in a single firm. Introduced in the 1985 book *Competitive Advantage*.

### Value investing

A capital management strategy based on acting on the observation of a clear difference between price and worth.

### Vertically integrated

A description of a company active in several nodes of an industry *value chain*.

### Volatility

A common *asset* management proxy for *risk*, broadly defined as the average daily change in the price of a security over the last month.

### Weakness

*Akrasia* in the form of capitulation after deliberation.

### Windfallapathy bias*

A cognitive tendency brought on by unexpected wealth that encourages indiscriminate investing.

### Write-down

A decrease in the *book value* of an *asset* through the recognition of an irregular expense on the income statement.

# BIBLIOGRAPHY

Cialdini, Robert B. *Influence: The Psychology of Persuasion*. Rev. ed. New York: Harper Business, 2006.

Graham, Benjamin, Sidney Cottle, Roger F. Murray, and Frank E. Block. *Graham and Dodd's Security Analysis*. 5th ed. New York: McGraw-Hill, 1988.

Graham, Benjamin. *The Intelligent Investor*. 4th ed. New York: Harper & Row, 1973.

Graham, Benjamin, and David Dodd. *Security Analysis*. 6th ed. New York: McGraw-Hill, 2008.

Greenblatt, Joel. *The Little Book That Beats the Market*. Hoboken: Wiley, 2010.

Kahneman, Daniel, and Amos Tversky. "Prospect Theory: An Analysis of Decision Under Risk." *Econometrica* 47, no. 2 (March 1979): 263–92.

Klarman, Seth A. *Margin of Safety: Risk-Averse Value Investing Strategies for the Thoughtful Investor*. New York: HarperCollins, 1991.

Porter, Michael E. "The Five Forces That Shape Strategy." *Harvard Business Review*, January 2008, 28–40.

Swensen, David F. *Pioneering Portfolio Management: An Unconventional Approach to Institutional Investment*. Rev. ed. New York: Free Press, 2009.

# NOTES

## CHAPTER 1
1. Tweedy, Browne Company LLC, "What Has Worked in Investing: Studies of Investment Approaches and Characteristics Associated with Exceptional Returns," Revised 2009.
2. Rolfe Winkler, "Airbnb Raises Over $100 Million as It Touts Strong Growth," *Wall Street Journal*, November 20, 2015.
3. Kia Kokalitcheva, "Airbnb Raises $100 Million Only Months After Last Funding Round," *Fortune*, November 20, 2015.
4. Leslie Hook, "Airbnb Raises a Further $100m," *Financial Times*, November 20, 2015.
5. Gardner Russo & Gardner LLC, *FY15-Q4 Form 13F-HR for the Period Ending December 31, 2015* (filed February 11, 2016).

## CHAPTER 2
1. U.S. Bureau of Labor Statistics, "CPI Detailed Report: Data for February 2016," 2016.
2. Douglas Macmillan, "Sequoia's Payout in WhatsApp Deal Could Hit $3 Billion," *Wall Street Journal*, February 19, 2014.
3. National Venture Capital Association, "Venture Capital Outperformed Major Stock Indices During Third Quarter of 2014," January 30, 2015.
4. Cambridge Associates, *U.S. Venture Capital Index® and Selected Benchmark Statistics*, December 31, 2014.
5. Joseph Ciolli and Sofia Horta e Costa, "S&P 500 Erases Monthly Gain on Final Day of 2014 Trading," *Bloomberg*, December 31, 2014.
6. Michael Mackenzie, "Stocks, Bonds and Gold Among 2010 Winners," *Financial Times*, December 30, 2010.
7. General Motors Company, *2014 Annual Report*, 3, 7, 13.

## CHAPTER 3
1. Lauren Davidson, "Apple Is Now Worth More Than $700bn," *Telegraph*, November 25, 2014.

## CHAPTER 4

1. Ministère du Budget des Comptes publics de la Fonction Publique, *Explanatory Notice 5000NOT-EN.*
2. MSCI Inc., *2015 Form 10-K*, February 26, 2016, 6.

## CHAPTER 5

1. Horsehead Holding Corp., *2014 Form 10-K*, March 2, 2015, 1.
2. LVMH Moët Hennessy–Louis Vuitton, *2015 Annual Report*, 2016, 16–17.
3. Wal-Mart Stores, Inc, *2015 Form 10-K*, March 30, 2016, 8.
4. Vivint Solar, Inc; *2015 Form 10-K*; March 15, 2016, 1–2, 7, M-34.
5. Unilever PLC, *Annual Report and Accounts 2015*, 2016, 2.
6. Chico's FAS, Inc, *2015 Form 10-K*, March 8, 2016, 2.
7. Wal-Mart, 3.
8. Target Corporation, *2015 Form 10-K*, March 16, 2016, 1–76.
9. Avon Products, Inc, *2015 Form 10-K*, February 23, 2016, 1–4.
10. Equity Residential, *2015 Form 10-K*, February 25, 2016, 4, 7, 22.
11. Svenska Cellulosa Aktiebolaget SCA (publ), *Annual Report 2015*, March 21, 2016, 2, 65.
12. Wal-Mart, 9, 13.
13. Wal-Mart, 26.
14. Philip Morris International, Inc., *2015 Form 10-K*, February 17, 2016, 1, 2, 22.
15. Medtronic plc, "Medtronic Completes Acquisition of Covidien," January 26, 2015.
16. Sears Holdings Corporation, *2015 Form 10-K*, March 16, 2016, 56, 57, 97.
17. Peter Lynch, *One Up on Wall Street* (New York: Simon & Schuster, 1989), 41.
18. Wal-Mart Stores, Inc., "Wal-Mart Corporate," May 1, 2016, http://corporate.walmart.com.
19. Ibid.
20. Clas Ohlson AB, "Clas Ohlson to Open New Stores in Hamburg," June 10, 2015.
21. Berkshire Hathaway Inc., *1996 Annual Report*, Shareholder letter, February 28, 1997.

## CHAPTER 6

1. International Financial Reporting Standards Foundation, *Staff Paper: IFRS Interpretations Committee Meeting*, March 12–13, 2013, 3.
2. LinkedIn Corporation, *2015 Form 10-K*, February 12, 2016, 72–73, 76.
3. LinkedIn Corporation, *2014 Form 10-K*, February 12, 2015, 82–83.

## CHAPTER 7

1. Cisco Systems, Inc., *2014 Annual Report*, 2.
2. Cisco Systems, Inc., *2013 Annual Report*, 3.
3. Cisco Systems, Inc., *2012 Annual Report*, 4.
4. Cisco Systems, Inc., *2014 Form 10-K*, 73.
5. The Gap, Inc., *2011 Form 10-K*, March 26, 2012, 11.
6. *Code of Federal Regulations*, Commodity and Securities Exchanges, title 17, sec. 229.303.
7. International Accounting Standards Board, *IFRS 16: Leases*, January 2016, 90.
8. H&M Hennes & Mauritz AB, *Annual Report 2015*, 98.
9. The Gap, Inc., *2015 Form 10-K*, March 21, 2016, 34, 48, 50, 61.

## CHAPTER 8

1. Loblaw Companies Limited, *2013 Annual Report–Financial Review*, 8.
2. The Kroger Co., *2015 Form 10-K*, 16.
3. Ibid, 34–35.
4. Whole Foods Market, Inc., *2013 Form 10-K*, 36–37.
5. The Gap, Inc., *2015 Form 10-K*, March 21, 2016, 35, 61.

## CHAPTER 9

1. The Gap, Inc., Earnings Conference Call, February 25, 2016.
2. The Gap, Inc., *2015 Form 10-K*, March 21, 2016, 38.

## CHAPTER 10

1. The Gap, Inc., *2015 Form 10-K*, March 21, 2016, 16, 35, 38, 49, 65.

## CHAPTER 11

1. The Gap, Inc., *2015 Form 10-K*, March 21, 2016, 15, 56; *2013 Form 10-K*, March 24, 2014, 35, 49, 51; *2012 Form 10-K*, March 26, 2013, 21, 32, 33, 36, 45.

## CHAPTER 12

1. Delta Financial Corporation, *2006 Form 10-K*, March 9, 2007, 1, 13.
2. Delta Financial Corporation, *Form 8-K*, January 5, 2009, 2.
3. Michael E. Porter, "The Five Forces That Shape Strategy," *Harvard Business Review*, January 2008, 28.
4. West Marine, Inc., *2010 Form 10-K*, March 14, 2011, 28.
5. International Flavors & Fragrances Inc., *2015 Form 10-K*, March 1, 2016, 3, 56–58.
6. The Kraft Heinz Company, *2015 Form 10-K*, March 3, 2016, 3–4, 55.
7. Axis AB, *Year-End Report 2015*, 1–2, 5.

8. GameStop Corp., *2014 Form 10-K*, March 30, 2015, 8–9, 13, 15, 17, F-9.
9. Weyerhauser Company, *2015 Form 10-K*, February 17, 2016, 3, 7, 66.
10. Facebook, Inc., *2015 Form 10-K*, January 28, 2016, 5, 10.
11. Jang-Sup Shin, *The Economics of the Latecomers: Catching-Up, Technology Transfer and Institutions in Germany, Japan and South Korea* (Abingdon: Routledge, 1996), 105–107.
12. United States Steel Corporation, *2015 Form 10-K*, February 29, 2016, 20–29.
13. Kenneth C. and Jane P. Laudon, *Management Information Systems: Managing the Digital Firm* (New York, Pearson, 2004), 68–71.
14. Nestlé India Limited, *2015 Annual Report*, 19–20.
15. "MAGGI Noodles Gains Further, Leads Category with More Than 50% Market Share MAGGI Vegetable Atta Noodles and MAGGI Oats Noodles Re-launched," Nestlé India Limited press release, April 19, 2016.
16. Oracle Corporation, *2015 Form 10-K*, June 25, 2015, 3.
17. Rick Summer, "New Cloud Solutions and Switching Costs Will Help Oracle Prevent Software-Industry Disruption," *Morningstar, Inc. research note*, March 16, 2016.
18. Geberit AG, *2015 Annual Report*, 33, 159, 165, 174, 190.
19. United States Department of Justice, *Americans With Disabilities Act of 1990, As Amended*, Sec. 12183, 35.
20. California Labor Code, Sections 7300–7324.2
21. Kone Oyj, *2015 Financial Statements*, 9, 24.

## CHAPTER 13

1. H&M Hennes & Mauritz AB, *Annual Report 2015*, 102.
2. Ibid, 98.
3. Costco Wholesale Corporation, *Schedule 14A*, December 18, 2015, 8.
4. Richard Milne, "Karl-Johan Persson, Chief Executive, Hennes & Mauritz," *Financial Times*, May 19, 2014.
5. Twenty-First Century Fox, Inc., *2015 Schedule 14A*, September 29, 2015, 12, 15.
6. Cenveo, Inc., *2015 Form 10-K*, February 26, 2016, 6.
7. Infineon Technologies AG, *2009 Form 20-F*, December 8, 2009, 110.
8. The Swatch Group SA, *2015 Compensation Report*, 8.
9. Ibid, 7.
10. Ibid, 7.
11. The Swatch Group SA, *2015 Annual Report*, 204.
12. Ibid, 187.
13. Fossil Group, Inc., *2016 Proxy Statement*, April 14, 2016, 34.
14. Ibid, 34.

15. Ibid, 19.
16. Ibid, 4.
17. Swatch *2015 Annual Report*, 203.
18. Ibid.
19. Fossil *2016 Proxy Statement*, 43.
20. Swatch *2015 Annual Report*, 217.
21. Ibid., 170.
22. The Swatch Group SA, *2014 Annual Report*, 166, 196.
23. Fossil Group, Inc., *2015 Form 10-K*, 34.
24. Ibid, 53.
25. Swatch *2015 Annual Report*, 187.
26. Ibid., 170.
27. Fossil *2015 10-K*, 33.

## CHAPTER 14

1. "Microsoft to Acquire LinkedIn," Microsoft Corporation press release, June 13, 2016.
2. "Toshiba and KONE Corporation to Take Stake in One Another," Toshiba Corporation press release, December 20, 2001.
3. "Completion of Sale of Certain Shares Held by Toshiba Subsidiary," Toshiba Corporation press release, July 22, 2015.
4. Flowserve Corporation, *2015 Form 10-K*, February 18, 2016, 23, 58, 80.
5. Flowserve Corporation, *Q1 2016 Form 10-Q*, April 28, 2016, 2, 10.
6. Flowserve Corporation, *2014 Form 10-K*, February 17, 2015, 56.
7. Ibid, 75.
8. Ibid, 75.
9. Ibid, 74.
10. Ibid, 53.

## CHAPTER 15

1. Yahoo Finance, "Maui Land & Pineapple Company, Inc. (MLP)," https://finance.yahoo.com/quote/mlp, accessed May 3, 2016.
2. Graham, Benjamin and David Dodd, *Security Analysis: The Classic 1934 Edition* (New York: McGraw-Hill, 1934), 80.

## CHAPTER 16

1. Benjamin Graham and David Dodd, *Security Analysis: The Classic 1940 Edition* (New York: McGraw-Hill, 2002), 681.
2. Graham and Dodd, 530.
3. Benjamin Graham, *The Intelligent Investor: A Book of Practical Counsel* (New York: Harper, 1959), 41.

4. Amos Tversky and Daniel Kahneman, "Availability: A Heuristic for Judging Frequency and Probability," *Cognitive Psychology* 5, no. 2 (1973): 207–232.
5. Thomas Gilovich, Robert Vallone, and Amos Tversky, "The Hot Hand in Basketball: The Misperception of Random Sequences," *Cognitive Psychology* 17 (1985): 295–314.
6. Aristotle, *Nicomachean Ethics*, trans. C.D.C. Reeve (Indianapolis: Hackett Publishing Company, 2014), 123.

## CHAPTER 17
1. Roger Blitz and Leo Lewis, "Pound Tumbles to 30-year Low as Britain Votes Brexit," *Financial Times*, June 24, 2016.

## CHAPTER 19
1. Melanie Warner and Stuart Elliott, "Frothier Than Ever: The Tall Cold One Bows to the Stylish One," *New York Times*, August 15, 2005, C1.
2. Jack Ewing, "Volkswagen Stock Falls as Automaker Tries to Contain Fallout," *New York Times*, September 21, 2015.
3. "Sound the Retweet," *Economist*, October 12, 2013.

## CHAPTER 21
1. S&P Dow Jones Indices, "SPIVA US Scorecard," year-end 2015.

# INDEX

# ABOUT THE AUTHOR

**Kenneth Jeffrey Marshall** teaches value investing at Stanford University and at the Stockholm School of Economics. He also teaches asset management in the MBA program at the University of California, Berkeley. He holds a BA in economics from the University of California, Los Angeles, and an MBA from Harvard Business School. He splits his time between California and Sweden.

www.kennethjeffreymarshall.com